The Serpent and the Wave

The Serpent and the Wave

A Guide to Movement Meditation

~~~~

Jalaja Bonheim

Celestial Arts
Berkeley, California

Text and cover design by Nancy Austin
Cover art: detail from Nine Dragons *by Chen Jung, 1244.*
    Francis Gardner Curtis Fund. Courtesy Museum of Fine Arts, Boston.
Illustrations on pages 11, 29, 49, 75, 99, 125, 126, 144, 177, 191, 205, 223
    by Laurelin Remington-Wolf
All other illustrations by Fuzzy Randall
Proofreading by Sheri Lent
Composition by Wilsted & Taylor

FIRST PRINTING 1992

Library of Congess Cataloging-in-Publication Data

Bonheim, Jalaja.
    The serpent and the wave : a guide to movement meditation / Jalaja
Bonheim.
        p.   cm.
    ISBN 0-89087-657-6
    1. Meditation.   2. Movement, Psychology of.   I. Title.
    II. Title: Movement meditation.
    BL627.B66   1992
    248.3'4—dc20   91-38137
                                                    CIP

1   2   3   4   5   6   7   8   9   10   /   96   95   94   93   92

AUTHOR'S NOTE

IN THIS TEXT, certain spiritual concepts and phenomena, such as *the Being* and *All That Is,* have been capitalized to emphasize their spiritual rather than customary meaning. The pronouns *she* and *he* are used alternately to indicate the third-person singular.

Any moving's from the Mover,
Any love from the Beloved.

RUMI

*Dedicated to the Black Forest, and to the fragile
beauty of the Earth and all her creatures.*

ACKNOWLEDGMENTS

I WISH TO EXPRESS my heartfelt thanks and gratitude to Peter Beren for his enthusiastic support; to all the people at Celestial Arts who helped me give birth to this book, especially Nicole Geiger and Fuzzy Randall; to Diana Reiss for her editorial expertise; to Sherry Ruth Anderson for her encouragement and help; to Laurelin Remington-Wolf for her exquisite artwork; and to Skip, for sharing his love and laughter.

CONTENTS

LIST OF MOVEMENT MEDITATIONS

Introduction

Dance, when you're broken open.
Dance, if you've torn the bandage off.
Dance in the middle of the fighting.
Dance in your blood.
Dance, when you're perfectly free.

Struck, the dancers hear a tambourine inside them,
as a wave turns to foam on its very top, begin.

Maybe you don't hear that tambourine,
or the tree leaves clapping time.

Close the ears on your head
that listen mostly to lies and cynical jokes.
There are other things to hear and see:
dance-music and a brilliant city
inside the Soul.

RUMI

I STARTED MEDITATING through movement because I was tired of sitting still. At the age of twenty, hungry for spiritual knowledge, I desperately wanted to meditate, and so tried to sit: cross-legged, on *zafus*, on chairs, alone, and in meditation centers. It was impossible. Sitting felt like self-imposed martyrdom: slowly, my restlessness would well up until I leapt from my seat like a volcano erupting. But my longing for wholeness and intimacy with an inner lover, whose presence I dimly sensed, would not allow me to accept the verdict of failure. I knew that if meditation was about spiritual communion, it must be accessible to anyone. Surely spirituality could not be the sole possession of those who managed to sit still. So, in wrestling with stillness, I was led to the practice of movement meditation.

Fortunately, around the same time I was struggling to sit still, I also began to dance. Having been raised to think of myself as an intellectual, I certainly did not identify myself as a dancer—a fact I now consider fortunate. It allowed me to dance for the pure pleasure of it, with no thought of achievement. At first, as a university student in Freiburg, Germany, I frequented a dance club located right next to the town's Gothic cathedral. The club was a run-down place, full of hippies who didn't object to my dancing barefoot, which I soon discovered was the only way I really enjoyed dancing. The music was rock and roll, blasted out at full volume on tinny loudspeakers. But with all its shortcomings, this place became my temple, my place of ecstasy. Night after night I danced myself into a trance, entering a state in which all things appeared perfect and whole.

Leaving the club late at night, my ears ringing from the pounding rhythms, I would walk out into the quiet medieval town square. There the ancient cathedral—so enormous, so silent, so breathtakingly beautiful—towered over the sleeping town. In its awe-inspiring presence I intuitively sensed that the source of its beauty was that same source I touched upon in my dancing.

It never occurred to me to associate dancing with meditation or spiritual practice. But much later, after I had moved to England, an incident changed my view. While teaching English at a university there, I fell in love with classical Indian dance after watching the solo performance of a young

Southern Indian woman. I decided to study with her, and as we began she said to me: "This dance is meditation. If you want to do this, it must be your spiritual practice. Don't confuse it with entertainment. It is a Yoga, a way of yoking yourself to divine power, and it will change you more than you realize." I was taught the first movement of opening myself to God and to the infinite sky, of bending down to touch the earth with reverence and gratitude, and finally joining my palms in acknowledgement of the light within all beings. I was told to repeat this movement, without fail, before and after dancing. This was my first formal initiation into sacred movement.

From that time on, movement meditation became my path of communion with the realm of spirit. I have since then learned to sit as well. But I know that I must give myself permission to move before I can sit. I now believe that the struggle against the body is unfortunate and unnecessary, and that the body's desire to move, instead of being repressed, can serve as an initiation to the spiritual source of all movement. For movement, like breathing, is a flow of energy.

But where does the source of the flow lie? This is a question that must be explored with an open-minded attitude of unknowing. If we are to experience full embodiment, a state in which the body moves and functions in perfect union with the soul's purpose, then we must release our deepseated mistrust and fear of the body.

It is time to rediscover skillful ways of approaching the body as a vessel of spirit in our times—ways that honor and integrate the knowledge of all traditions but work with the psyche and the cultural conditioning of Western people. Though Indian dance for me has remained an important element of my spiritual practice, its ethnic and religious origins, as well as its complexity, limit its value as a spiritual discipline for most Westerners. We can profit from the study of Eastern methods—Tai Chi Ch'uan, Aikido, Kum Nye, or Hatha Yoga—but sooner or later we reach a barrier that lets us know it is time to find our own path. Captivating as the Eastern forms of movement meditation may be, they emerged within a social, cultural, and religious context completely different from our own. Not surprisingly, they fail to address many issues relevant to spiritual practice in an urban Western society. It is very important to consider carefully what kind of movement we need to balance ourselves energetically. This varies a great deal according to the individual's environment, lifestyle, constitution, and type of work.

My own way of movement meditation evolved gradually through working both alone and with many individuals and groups. "What do you do in your groups?" has always been a difficult question to answer. There is no set format, and never have any two workshops been alike. Often we move in conjunction with other practices: dance flows into stillness, into emotional processing, into chanting, prayer, bodywork, or art. A certain meditation is never repeated twice in quite the same way. I hope you will use the written meditations as starting points to take off on your own and perhaps to start your own movement meditation circles. I feel that we have too often allowed our creativity—and, above all, our relationship to God—to be imprisoned by traditionally defined formal structures. Therefore, although I use many forms in my work, I suggest that we continually allow them to dissolve back into the flow again so that we can be empty and open to the next step.

First, we might stand in a circle. The chatter dies down, replaced by a sense of listening. The dancers listen, and the drummer listens. Then, perhaps, very softly, a beat emerges out of the silence—the heartbeat—and our feet begin to stamp it, first one person, then others joining in, until we are linked in the rhythm. This is the seed. Now the circle takes off and unfolds on its own, depending on the energies of those present, the environment, the atmosphere, the season.

Perhaps the rhythms inspire a sound or a chant, or we find our arms being drawn toward the center. As we reach out, our fingertips spark a pillar of fire that surges up through the circle's center, while our feet hold the earth's heartbeat. Cradling this flame in our hands, we let it stream through our arms, our hearts, our bellies, and begin to raise the tongues of fire into the sky.

Who knows what will happen next? An individual may claim the center space, the sanctified space, for her bodyprayer. Another may begin to spin through space, dancing in ways he never knew he could, filled trembling with a sense of presence. Such are the times when—though one may never have thought of oneself as a dancer—the most exquisite, perfectly choreographed dances emerge without giving any thought to the matter at all.

At times I will give voice to the images that flow through me as I move, entering a light trance. When people are in a state of harmony and meditative receptivity, the group spirit itself creates the meditation needed in that moment; my role is merely to be open and allow the images, the movements, and the silence beneath them to flow through. Perhaps we will repeat the simple steps of a sacred dance over and over, dancing for a long time, moving through boredom and exhaustion and resistance. Finally we become one with the rhythm, we *are* the rhythm, in perfect harmony with the innumerable precise rhythms of nature, with the heartbeat of the drums, with our own heartbeat and the heartbeat of the earth.

As we move together in conscious, gentle ways, participants frequently comment that what we are doing feels extremely ancient. They also describe experiencing the earth in ways they never had before, as if it had suddenly come alive, no longer inert matter, but a sacred, living miracle.

Indeed, many of us are aware that unless we learn to honor the earth's sanctity, we may be destined to be strangled by our own garbage and pollution. In these times, no one can ignore the fragility of this planet or the immense suffering that human ignorance is inflicting upon all creatures. Unless we renew a sense of humility that can honor the interdependence of everything within creation, we are destined for annihilation. The practice of movement meditation allows us, in a very natural and effortless way, to make the step from this theoretical knowledge to the actual experience of the sacredness of all bodies. I pray that our dance be one of transformation, of healing, and of rekindling our sense of awe for the miracle of life.

CHAPTER ONE

Remembering

All Bibles or sacred codes have been the causes of the following Errors.

1. That Man has two real existing principles Viz: a Body & a Soul.
2. That Energy, calld Evil, is alone from the Body, & that Reason, calld Good, is alone from the Soul.
3. That God will torment Man in Eternity for following his Energies.

But the following Contraries to these are True

1. Man has no Body distinct from his Soul for that calld Body is a portion of Soul discerned by the five Senses, the chief inlets of Soul in this age.
2. Energy is the only life and is from the Body and Reason is the bound or outward circumference of Energy.
3. Energy is eternal Delight.

WILLIAM BLAKE

The Rapture of Movement

To lose oneself in the rapture of movement and enter states of heightened presence, trance, or ecstasy is quite natural. Children do so all the time and in their play rediscover the most ancient ways of altering consciousness. What child has not twirled around until she felt like the still center of a spinning universe, or endlessly repeated a simple motion until she went into trance? In the West, we tend to disregard these activities as mere play. But in other parts of the world, people have carefully observed and charted the effects of movement on the human mind and spirit. Movement meditation is a conscious continuation of this journey into our bodies, into ourselves.

Movement meditation belongs to a vast spiritual heritage in which serpent and wave imagery plays a central part. However, to a large extent, this heritage has been expelled from the Jewish, Christian, and Islamic traditions. As you begin to practice movement meditation, you will probably experience the power of wave and serpentine movements, and you may intuitively grasp their profound significance. You may also find yourself wondering why such an obvious gateway to states of expanded consciousness was never mentioned in your own religious upbringing, and you may question old beliefs concerning the nature and relationship of body and spirit. This chapter will discuss the greater religious and philosophical context out of which our individual experience emerges.

What Is the Body?

Because Western religion has discouraged the cultivation of body consciousness, the idea of movement as a form of spiritual practice is still as unfamiliar—and as outlandish—as the idea that enlightenment might be a physical state as much as a mental and spiritual one. Our heritage includes an attitude of basic distrust of the body that goes all the way back to the apostle Paul's declaration that no permanent reconciliation between body and spirit is possible: "The desires of the flesh are against the spirit, and the desires of the spirit are against the flesh."

Contemporary poet Robert Bly points out that even today the following words are spoken in each Christian Science service:

> There is no life, truth, substance, nor intelligence in matter. All is infinite mind, and its infinite manifestation, for God is all in all.
> Spirit is immortal truth; matter is mortal error. Spirit is real, and eternal; matter is unreal and temporal.
> Spirit is God, and man is his image and likeness. Therefore man is not material, he is spiritual.[1]

When the body's spiritual essence is denied, movement ceases to be treasured as a vehicle for passage into the realm of the sacred. How often have we heard it said that the body must be transcended in order to experience spiritual truth? How often has the body been equated with separation and illusion, as opposed to the "higher" knowledge of the spirit!

The problem is partly conceptual. According to most Eastern medical and spiritual systems, we have not one but many bodies, or one body with many layers. These are sometimes called the physical, astral, and causal bodies, while other teachings distinguish between five, seven, or even more layers that range from the physical to the emotional, mental, and spiritual dimensions. But when Western texts speak of the body, they generally refer to the body as perceived through the physical senses only. This perception is not only incomplete but is also distorted by the mind's projections. According to most esoteric traditions, the body can be perceived accurately through the inner eye alone, never through the outer senses. Our attachment to surface appearances blocks our view of an integrated reality. If by "body" we refer only to what our outer senses perceive, then we will indeed find it an inadequate vehicle for spiritual experience. But if we can release these mental limitations and practice moment-by-moment awareness of embodied experience, we will discover that our body is in fact an ever-present gateway into ecstasy.

Most traditional cultures share a common belief that the body, far from being an obstacle to spiritual realization, can be an invaluable tool, provided we know how to use it correctly. These cultures would consider it impossible to conduct a successful ritual, healing, or worship ceremony without including sacred movement or dance. In all Eastern and shamanic traditions, mental and emotional preparation of the spiritual seeker are combined with intensive bodywork and exercise. All these traditions have developed highly refined forms of movement meditation, such as shamanic dancing in the Native American traditions, various forms of trance dancing in the Middle East, Tai Chi in China, Hatha Yoga and Tantra Yoga in India, Aikido in Japan, or Kum Nye in Tibet, all of which use the body as a spiritual tool. Such treasures of insight into the secrets of moving energy are not garnered casually. Rather, they are deliberately accumulated over many centuries, and invariably the process is supported by a mythology that teaches people to value the physical body and encourages the cultivation of body awareness.

The Mythology of Oneness

A comparison of Western religion with Eastern and shamanic spiritual traditions reveals two very different philosophical and religious approaches: the *mythology of dualism* and the *mythology of oneness*.

As the name implies, myths of oneness assume that everything in existence, everything in the universe is one. The notion of a many-dimensional body belongs to a more holistic view of existence, in which the material and the spiritual are opposites only insofar as they represent opposite polarities along the single spectrum of All That Is. And as in a hologram, the entire spectrum is present within every atom of our bodies. All dualities are only of relative significance; as a year encompasses both summer and winter, so existence encompasses both matter and spirit. Ultimately, everything in the universe is one, and everything is interdependent. Within the single gigantic organism of the universe, the pairs of opposites are engaged in a continuous dance of transformation. As summer turns into winter, and winter into summer, so matter can dissolve into spirit, and spirit may solidify as matter.

The image of the serpent lies at the heart of this universal mythology

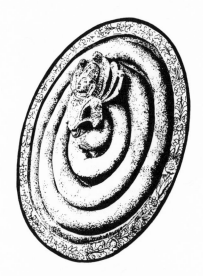

The great serpent king of the underworld.
Temple of Badami, India, 6th century.

of oneness. In every aspect of its being, the serpent reveals to us the concept of two-in-one, with its movement that undulates between right and left, its venom that can both harm and heal, its habit of reemerging, as if reborn, from the husk of a dead skin. Associated with innumerable deities, both male and female, the serpent represents the pulsation between the opposite polarities that is the source of all creation. As we shall see later, meditation on the serpentine and wavelike movements of our own bodies is extremely powerful. Not only do serpents and waves represent the most elemental pattern of moving energy, visible in the play of wind, sand, and ocean, but these movements also function as a doorway into the experience of spiritual oneness.

In the context of the mythology of oneness, even such terms as *spirit* and *body* are misleading, based as they are on dualistic concepts. Instead, Indian philosophy speaks of Shakti and Shiva. Shakti, the name of the Great Goddess, is given to all manifestations of physical energy—wind, electricity, nuclear power, the atom. Present within both men and women, Shakti is inseparable from her lover Shiva, who is pure consciousness. Thus, while both Shakti and Shiva are spirit, Shakti is manifest whereas Shiva is unmanifest. All matter is the body of Shakti, her sacred, mysterious form, and so, each body is to be equally respected and cherished, whether it be the body of a human, an animal, or a mountain. This is a concept of clear and profound significance in the context of ecology. Omnipresent, Shakti disguises herself as inert matter, as dull and unconscious. And yet, hidden within the heaviness of a stone is her eternal light-essence. In this way, the ancient Indians, like many other cultures, recognized the unity of existence many millennia ago.

Myths of oneness assume that all creatures are of divine origin in both body and spirit. They tend to describe creation as a process whereby the one divides into many so that each fragment is a complete microcosmic reflection of all the creator's aspects. Some stories describe how the primal Being is quite literally dismembered, while others say that it broke into an original couple, male and female, who then cocreated the world. The Brahadaranyaka Upanishad, an Indian text dated around 700 B.C.E., says that at some point, the one, infinite Being began to feel lonely. Longing for love, it divided into two, male and female, and in this way began to make love to itself. Thus the female gave birth to the human race. Then she proceeded to play a game of hide-and-seek with her lover: when she hid in the body of a cow, he became a bull, and together they produced the race of cattle. She became a horse, a goat, a swallow, an insect; whatever form she took, he also took, and thus they created all the species that now inhabit the earth.[2]

Such myths celebrate the divine essence within the myriad phenomena of the universe. They teach us to honor our bodies and all creation as sacred. The molecules of our bodies are those of the divine body and contain dormant potential for enlightened consciousness. The challenge of embodied existence is to recognize the light of the one divine Being as it shines through the opacity of material form, and to remember the body's true nature as a manifestation of divine energy or light. Thus we become one with the power that created us by virtue of having realized our true nature.

The Body of Light

While in other parts of the world the continuity of spiritual practice was continually disrupted by the turmoil of wars, invasions, and migrations, Tibetan culture until quite recently evolved in extreme geographic isolation. This long period of peaceful, uninterrupted cultural evolution has allowed the interplay of body and spirit to be studied and meditated upon more thoroughly in Tibet than anywhere else, supporting millennia of fruitful experimentation along the borderlands of matter and spirit.

Various Tibetan spiritual teachings hold that one can learn to communicate with the body at the cellular and molecular level in order to heighten its vibrational frequency. Through highly esoteric meditations, the body's material substance is awakened to its true nature, described—as in many other traditions—as light, spirit, or pure vibrational energy. The fully awakened body can, like light itself, manifest either in the form of material particles, or as nonmaterial wave-energy, since the true nature of the body is light or vibration. Along similar lines, the Indian master Paramahansa Yogananda compares the physical world to a movie image that would vanish without a trace if the projector were to be switched off—the projector being God, the source of light. Both energy and matter, he says, are essentially spirit in motion.[3]

Namkhai Norbu, one of the great living Tibetan Buddhist masters, says that the practice of manifesting what is called the *body of light* or the *rainbow body* continues in Tibet to the present day. Norbu's account of one such case provides a clear example of the intensely physical nature of spiritual practices based on myths of oneness. This story concerns a famous master who had previously announced his intention to die:

> The monastery spread the news far and wide that this man had said that he wanted to be left closed up for seven days to die, and since everyone understood the significance of this, many people came, and the whole thing became a public event. There were representatives of all the various Buddhist schools, from the great monasteries, and even members of the Chinese administration, who at that time were all military personnel. Thus, when they opened the room in which the man had been locked for seven days, there were many people present. And what they saw was that the man had left no body. Only his hair and nail, the impurities of the body, were left.[4]

A similar case involved the death of Norbu's uncle. After having his disciples sew him into a tent, he is said to have dissolved his body into rainbow light, leaving behind nothing but hair, nails, and clothing.

The Western mind will certainly find these stories alien, for they challenge the deepest beliefs we hold about the nature of body and spirit. And yet for this very reason they are important stories to contemplate. Movement meditation also starts from the assumption that we truly do not know what our body is. It requires us to stay open-minded to the possibility that our body may have other dimensions than the one visible to our physical eyes.

It is interesting that Christian tradition describes a phenomenon similar to the Tibetan body of light. Jesus is said to have ascended to heaven not merely in spirit, but with his physical body. In discussing the seeming miracle of a physical body dissolving into light, Namkhai Norbu explains that reality is a void, a blank mirror. We mistake the physical objects that appear in this mirror to be real, though they are in truth mere light shows, images without substance:

> To use the metaphor of the mirror once again, this realization of the Body of Light means that one is no longer in the condition of the reflections, but has entered the condition of the mirror itself, and moved into the nature and energy of the mirror.[5]

Where Western religion teaches that spirit inhabits the body like a temporary hotel room, the goal of Tibetan spiritual practice is a true union of body and spirit.

Gender Associations

While extreme Christian doctrine has declared war against the human body, other more moderate voices advise us to honor the body as the temple of spirit or the vessel of the soul. But why assume that the body is merely a useful but spiritually insignificant container? Why do we cling so tenaciously to the concept of body and spirit as two separate entities? And why do we unfailingly associate the serpent force with evil? These questions can only be answered by looking carefully at the role of gender associations and patriarchal beliefs in the Western spiritual tradition. As we shall see, the relationship between men and women and the relationship between spirit and matter run parallel.

The association of man with spirit and woman with the body appears at least as early as Aristotle's *Politics;* it remains a constant theme throughout the Middle Ages.[6] The Latin word *spiritus,* root of the English word *spirit,* takes the masculine form, while *matter* is feminine, derived from the Latin *mater,* or mother. Western tradition also associates the masculine with intellect, rationality, transcendence, the sky, and the sun, while the feminine has been linked with emotions, intuition, immanence, the earth, and the moon.

In the meditations in this text, I speak of the earth in the feminine gender as mother-earth, and of the sky in the masculine gender as father-sky. In general, Western cultural history has established the earth-mother and sky-father as permanent archetypes in our consciousness. Yet in recognizing and making use of these archetypes we must not ascribe universal validity to them: we should remember that all gender associations are culture specific, and even deeply ingrained archetypes such as mother-earth and father-sky are not universally shared. In Egypt, for example, the sky goddess Nut was complemented by her earth-brother Geb. And though current Western cultural association depicts the sun as masculine and the moon feminine, the modern German language still reflects the consciousness of an earlier culture that considered the moon masculine and the sun feminine.

Throughout time, human beings have projected gender associations onto deities, nature forces, and inanimate objects. Many women today feel uncomfortable with traditional definitions of the feminine. The root of the problem lies not so much in the definitions themselves but in the fact that our culture has forgotten the vital importance of sexual equality—not only as a social value but as an important gateway to spiritual wholeness. Both in the outer world and within, male and female energies must be balanced, for regardless of how the masculine and feminine qualities are defined, both represent aspects that every man and every woman embody. In all myths of oneness, both are honored equally. Indeed, many early Christians such as the Gnostics regarded God as an androgynous being.[7]

When Western gender associations are compounded with the misogyny inherent in patriarchal thought and monotheism based on an exclusively male god, we are left with a legacy of deep-rooted imbalance. Patriarchal ideology today continues to have a destructive influence, not so much because of how it defines the masculine and the feminine principles, but because it denies their equal value. What is needed today is no simple reversal of gender associations—though this, too, may occur—but a rebalancing of the feminine and the masculine within ourselves and within society.

Movement meditation requires a direct encounter and reconciliation with everything that our tradition associates with the feminine and consequently devalues. When you begin to consciously work with your body, you may discover all kinds of judgments. Your body may seem disgusting, imperfect, chaotic, unreliable, or embarrassing to you. Since in our tradition the body has been associated with the feminine, men have suffered the effects of this aspect of self-alienation to an even greater degree than women. The body brings us face to face with nature and sexuality, with cyclical change and the eternal state of flux that characterizes of physical existence.

Patriarchal forms of spiritual practice tend to impose strict controls on all bodily functions. Ultimately the body cannot be controlled: it sweats and oozes and excretes and ages moment by moment. Western religion has tried to insulate God in a realm of strict abstract perfection where he could remain untouched by the messiness of bodily existence. As a result, our God has no dance, no rhythm, no cycles, no body. He is divorced from life on earth, from the seasons of nature and the cycles of birth and death. Here the shimmering, oscillating, earthbound serpent becomes the devil's ally, the incarnation of evil, a force that leads us to confuse good and evil, right and wrong, matter and spirit. While Western religion has embraced the notion of transcendence of earthly matters, serpentine myths of oneness lead us to the divine not by rejecting the rhythms and passions of embodied life, but by penetrating to their very essence and finding in the heart of the dance the still center of infinity.

The Reign of Patriarchy

Western civilization was not always patriarchal. Archaeological evidence, much of which was excavated only in the last few decades, has shown that prehistoric men and women throughout Europe, the Middle East, and Asia worshipped the Great Goddess in many forms. Archaeologists have traced goddess worship back to the Neolithic communities of about 7000 B.C.E. and further back to the Upper Paleolithic cultures that existed around 25,000 B.C.E., according to Merlin Stone.[8]

Some three or four millennia ago, tribes of migrating northern warriors invaded Europe. Waves of invasions continued to occur over the next several thousand years, and the invaders brought male gods and male-dominated social structures with them. Over the next millennia, goddess worship gradually succumbed to the new patriarchal myths and religions. In some cases, names, festivals, and rituals of the Goddess were incorporated into patriarchal religions. For example, Christmas was originally the time in which the rebirth of the light—the winter solstice—was celebrated by erecting a tree, ancient symbol of the Goddess.[9] In other cases, the rituals and rites of goddess worship were brutally suppressed. As Merlin Stone points out, the Old Testament contains many references to the wholesale slaughter of goddess-worshippers by the Hebrews. Old myths of oneness began to be slowly replaced by myths of dualism. These have provided the foundation for the Judeo-Christian-Islamic tradition and so for the entire structure of Western culture over the last two thousand years. Hand in hand with the suppression of the Goddess came a radical revision of women's position and power in society; from that era forward, women were forced to be subordinate to men.

The suppression of goddess worship in favor of an ideology based on male supremacy was not a sudden event, but a gradual process. By the time of Jesus' birth, patriarchy had established a solid presence throughout Europe. In the centuries after his death the growing Christian church evolved into a bulwark of patriarchal authority. Elaine Pagels, professor of religious studies at Princeton University, describes how in the process of its consolidation, the Church expelled numerous dissident voices and thoroughly purged the Bible of all references to the feminine aspects of God:

> Every one of the secret texts which gnostic groups revered was omitted from the canonical collection, and branded as heretical by those who called themselves orthodox Christians. By the time the process of sorting the various writings ended—probably as late as the year 200—virtually all the feminine imagery for God had disappeared from orthodox tradition.[10]

> By the year 200, the majority of Christian communities endorsed as canonical the pseudo-Pauline letter of Timothy, which stresses (and exaggerates) the anti-feminist element in Paul's views: "Let a woman learn in silence with all submissiveness. I permit no woman to teach or to have authority over men: she is to keep silent." . . . By the end of the second century, women's participation in worship was explicitly condemned: groups in which women continued on to leadership were branded as heretical.[11]

We must understand clearly that the gradual takeover of patriarchy was a global, and not merely a Western, phenomenon. China, for example, underwent a similar shift from matriarchy to patriarchy, as did India and the entire Middle East. Recognizing the misogyny and body-denial in their upbringing, many modern Western people mistakenly assume that by leaving Christianity they will leave old repressive patterns behind. But this is not the case. Religions are not static; they develop and change along with the society that supports them. Christianity is not the only religion in which the original teachings have been distorted and corrupted. The shift that Christianity underwent—from the original spiritual inspiration to increasingly sexist and hierarchical values—also took place in Buddhism, Hinduism, and most notably in Islam. All Asian religions are today being handed down in the context of staunchly patriarchal societies in which sexual repression, the oppression of women, and misogyny run rampant. The result is that many Eastern spiritual traditions have incorporated anti-feminine elements that coexist side by side with goddess worship.

The War on Dance

Throughout the centuries, a number of Christian churches have waged a veritable war on dance, struggling to banish dance and movement from spiritual practice. When we dance, the serpent, ancient enemy of the orthodox, raises its head; enthralled by the music, it begins to dance with us. The undulating serpentine movements of our own bodies represent one of the most powerful tools we possess for achieving a state of "at-oneness" with existence. To dance is to open wide the doors to the very forces that, though worshipped in pre-Christian times, were later associated with witchcraft and devils and were banished into the nether regions of hell.

Early Christians, in fact, were well acquainted with the power of moving with the spirit. By the third and fourth centuries, however, the church was firmly entrenched in its anti-feminine and anti-physical attitude, and dance was condemned as a direct path to damnation. Even today, certain Christian sects have not come all that far from the fanaticism of Bishop Johannes Chrystostomos, who in the fourth century C.E. declared:

> Where there is dance, there the devil will also be present. For God gave us feet, not so that we might dance, but so that we might walk on the straight path; not so that we be uncontrolled and not for us to jump around like camels (for they, too, not only women, do their disgusting dances), but so that we join the choir of angels.[12]

In the Middle Ages, churchmen still tolerated certain dances that they deemed "pure" but banished all dancing that might arouse the passions they were so committed to subduing. From about 1700 onward, all dance was categorically denounced as inappropriate activity for a good Christian: "Neither the Roman Catholic church nor the Protestant Christian churches allowed sacred dances in their services."[13]

But what we repress becomes part of the psyche's shadow. Hell is what we create when we repress, distort, and pervert the primal forces of nature. Through repression the good Christian developed a dark shadow that would at times violently break loose and possess his body in the form of devils and goblins. Try as they might to control themselves, medieval Christians were sometimes literally forced to participate in wild, out-of-control dance frenzies. The history of the Middle Ages describes eruptions of mysterious dance manias that swept through Europe like epidemics, compelling people to dance until they collapsed. Kaye Hoffman, in her book *Tanz, Trance, and Transformation,* quotes several medieval German accounts of such occurrences.[14] In 1374, people in the Rhein-Mosel area entered mysterious states of trance in which they danced until they collapsed. This dance mania spread until there were hordes of dancers traveling from one town to the next—five hundred of them alone in the city of Cologne—who begged for money for their sustenance and were considered a public nuisance, especially since there were many unmarried women among them. These women, the narrator indignantly claims, all became pregnant due to the immorality associated with dance. In another instance, more than one hundred children spontaneously gathered in the town of Erfurt, fell into a trance, and began to dance, while their parents looked on in shock, unable to restrain them.

The church quite accurately recognized the serpentine nature of these dance frenzies and repeatedly condemned them as the work of the devil. In the midst of such irresistible compulsions, the same power erupted that, in more accepting societies, was evoked without fear in order to purposefully move into states of trance. Dance, as an expression of serpent power, bridges the conscious and the unconscious realms, allowing the often-separated dimensions of reality to meet and interweave. But where ecstasy and the expression of the unconscious forces are forbidden, these energies will violently force their way to the surface.

In many European folk songs and stories, the memory of these events lingers on:

> Once upon a time there was a king who had twelve daughters, each
> more beautiful than the other. They slept together in a hall where their
> beds stood close to one another. At night when they had gone to bed,
> the King locked the door and bolted it. But when he unlocked it in the

morning, he noticed that their shoes had been danced to pieces, and nobody could explain how it happened.[15]

So begins a Brothers Grimm tale, one of many in which an irresistible dance mania takes over, generally explained as the work of magic, devils, or other creatures of the dark underworld. In the fairy tale above, the princesses dance the night away in an underground castle with seven enchanted princes. Suffocated by the restraints of Christian morality, the psyche escapes into a nighttime world in which men and women join in a dance of love—a place where dance, sexuality, and pleasure reign supreme. However, the prevalent morality of nineteenth-century man cannot condone such goings-on. The hero is summoned to stop the illicit parties, and the princes are punished: "But for every night that the underground princes had spent in dancing with the princesses, a day was added to their time of enchantment."

Orthodox Christianity has yet to deal openly or consciously with its distrust of the feminine or its rejection of the body. Sadly, even today the Catholic church does not recognize dance as a legitimate form of spiritual expression and continues to excommunicate priests who introduce dance into mass. As recently as 1989, Matthew Fox, the director of the Institute in Culture and Creation Spirituality, was silenced by the church because of his sympathy and support for feminist and body-affirming teachings. In his book, *The Coming of the Cosmic Christ,* he demands:

> BRING THE BODY BACK. The body has been effectively banished from most white worship in the West. That is one role stationary benches play in the churches—they assure that no dance, no celebration of body-spirit, might break loose. Books play a similar role in worship— if people have to hold books, then their hands are also occupied and they aren't free to move the body. But there can be no living worship without the body.[16]

As one of my movement meditation students said, recalling childhood memories: "Church was a place where you had to put away your body when you walked in the door." All too easily, organized religion's core of inner truth is shrouded by veils of shame, guilt, and repressive conditioning, as a sturdy tree may be smothered by parasites. But Christianity need no longer be a patriarchal religion. Patriarchy and the suppression of the feminine have no basis in the original teachings of Jesus, which were later edited and adapted to the needs of the evolving church. On the contrary, Jesus appears to have been a radical egalitarian, to whom men and women alike were children of God. Many of the virtues Jesus emphasized, such as compassion, tenderness, gentleness, and love, are, by the standards of Western civilization, feminine values. In his teachings there is no evidence whatsoever of the anti-feminine and anti-physical attitudes of the later Christian church.

We have inherited both the wisdom and the ignorance of our ancestors; we ourselves must initiate the process of renewal and like the serpent shed the old, worn-out skins. It is time once again to approach our own bodies with wonder and respect, renewing our sense of reverence for the sacred world we inhabit.

Rediscovering the Serpentine Way

It is not accidental that the West is now rediscovering the ancient myths of oneness. The popularization of the new scientific research has contributed immensely to a growing realization that Western materialism, for all its alleged objectivity, may be missing the whole truth. As philosopher Ken Wilber says, "Classical science was destined to be self-liquidating."[17] Physicist Fritjof Capra claims that "the basic oneness of the universe is not only the central characteristic of the mystical experience, but is also one of the most important revelations of modern physics."[18] Indeed, the scientific exploration of the subatomic world has initiated a radical revision of contemporary conceptions of physical reality, and many ancient mystical teachings now seem uncannily modern, as Capra has written:

> Quantum theory forces us to see the universe not as a collection of physical objects, but rather as a complicated web of relations between the various parts of a unified whole. This, however, is the way in which

Eastern mystics have experienced the world, and some of them have expressed their experience in words which are almost identical with those used by atomic physicists.[19]

Simultaneously, our approach to spirituality and spiritual practice is undergoing an equally profound transformation. In the majority of Western churches, communal worship is still mediated by the priesthood, rather than participatory or tribal, and the body, like the congregation, is strictly controlled and forced to play a purely passive role. Nonetheless, new forms of worship and sacred play are bubbling up everywhere.

Movement meditation itself belongs to the tradition of tantric mysticism, which allows every individual to commune with the sacred, reverentially honoring all manifestations of energy, including sexuality, anger, and grief. The reemergence of movement meditation in the West is merely one aspect of a greater transformation leading toward a new relationship with our bodies, with the feminine, and with the earth. A new mythology is emerging that encourages us to relate to our bodies as vehicles of transformation and enlightenment. Not only are women reclaiming their power, but many men too are searching for different images of maleness and a different kind of strength than their fathers taught them—the strength to be tender, vulnerable, fluid, and sensual. These are aspects of God represented in Pan, Dionysus, and Krishna, aspects long denied in our own culture.

In reclaiming the body as an instrument of spiritual evolution, we are placing ourselves in the lineage of all mystic traditions—the Sufis within the Islamic tradition; the visionaries such as Master Eckhart, Hildegard von Bingen, or Matthew Fox in the Christian tradition; the lovers of the Shekinah in the Jewish tradition; Mirabai and Kabir in India. These were the ones who honored the feminine aspect of God, and in doing so, honored nature as the physical manifestation of the feminine. These were the dancers, the singers, and often the outcasts, the rebels wrestling against the mainstream. It is their heritage that we are awakening to in our twentieth-century way, when we arise and invite our body to speak.

CHAPTER TWO

Beginning the Journey

The Guest is inside you, and also inside me;
you know the sprout is hidden inside the seed.
We are all struggling; none of us has gone far.
Let your arrogance go, and look around inside.

The blue sky opens out farther and farther,
the daily sense of failure goes away,
the damage I have done to myself fades,
a million suns come forward with light,
when I sit firmly in that world.

KABIR
AS ADAPTED BY ROBERT BLY

Movement Meditation Is for Everyone

ANYONE CAN PRACTICE movement meditation—young or old, people in wheelchairs and dancers. If you are alive, you move, and if you move, you can meditate on your movements. The most pleasurable movements are usually very simple ones: a ballet performance certainly provides a spectacular sight for the audience, but a traditional African folk dance may be a far more fulfilling experience for the dancers themselves. In beginning movement meditation, the first step is to affirm to yourself: "I am moving for myself, for my own pleasure. This is a gift to me!" When you understand this, there is no pressure to "do it right" to please the instructor or even your own inner critic.

Claiming Your Authority

The word *authority* comes from Greek *authos,* meaning self; authority means power over yourself, or empowerment of the self. Since religion so often tells us exactly how we are to handle our body—what we are to eat or not eat, whether and how and when to be sexually active—it leaves us particularly prone to handing over our power to others in the area of spiritual practice. Many of us were taught to believe in a god who, as the ultimate authority figure, would approve or disapprove of our actions and reward or punish us accordingly.

But spirituality—as opposed to religion—is a highly individual, undogmatic, and democratic adventure, open to everyone without exception. Though you may feel confused and unsure of yourself, you are your own teacher. Somewhere inside, you know exactly how your spirit wants to move, and the first step is to claim your authority.

Unfortunately, most education teaches us to ignore or distrust our own experience. We are taught how *not* to move, how *not* to trust our body, how to be more concerned with outward appearance than inner feelings. By contrast, all forms of sacred movement focus on inner experience more than on

Dancing in honor of the god Apollo, Greek
vase, 410 B.C.E.

outer appearances. Even in the presence of an audience, the dancer's state
of consciousness is more important than the visual effect.

In dancing, your own experience matters, not the experience of any potential observer. Whenever you move with pleasure, you stop comparing
yourself with others. The question is no longer, "How good do I look?
How well am I performing? How will I be perceived?"; rather it is, "How
good does this movement feel?" Because true pleasure is rooted in your individual uniqueness, it is by its very nature anti-authoritarian and a good
indicator of whether a movement is appropriate to you.

Social discipline almost always involves some degree of repressive conditioning. Although such training may function as a stepping stone into
spiritual discipline, it also represents a wound from which we must heal. To
some extent, during the process of socialization, we have all received messages that our natural way of being was insufficient or even downright bad.
These messages must be transcended before we can manifest spiritual discipline. Out of touch with our bodies, we are easily convinced that we need
experts—doctors and cosmeticians, color consultants, fitness and nutri-
tional specialists—to make decisions for us. However, although we may
value an expert's advice, in the end we ourselves are best equipped to make
our own decisions. According to the radical Indian spiritual teacher, J.
Krishnamurti:

When we understand ourselves, the authority of any specialist, psychosociological or any other, comes to an end. I feel this must be understood by each one of us before we go any further. Because most of us, unfortunately, are slaves to other people's ideas. Most of us are so easily persuaded, influenced by the specialist, by authority. Especially when we are going into this question of understanding ourselves, which is of primary importance, there is no authority whatsoever, because you have to understand yourself and not somebody else or what somebody else says about you.[1]

The Example of the Buddha

The impulse to take leave of tradition and find one's own path is as old as religion itself. Many religious founders were themselves rule-breakers—nonconformists willing to relinquish what they had learned in order to return to a state of innocence and unknowing. All spiritual masters, Buddha and Jesus among them, realized that the ancient ways, although sacred, must change if their original spirit is not to be lost.

The life of the Buddha provides a wonderful example of a human being who went beyond all rules to find his own authority. His teachers instructed him in detail concerning the use of the body; their doctrine held that bodily needs were to be ignored and transcended. Contemporary Vietnamese Buddhist teacher Thich Nhat Hanh tells how once, after weeks of fasting and self-deprivation, Siddhartha, the Buddha, fainted. A peasant woman found him and offered him a bowl of fresh milk. Although his teachers had forbidden him to drink milk, the Buddha accepted it, and after drinking, said:

> "Please give me another bowl of milk." Because he saw that the milk was doing wonderful things, and he knew that once our body is strong enough, we can succeed in meditation. . . .
>
> The five other monks Siddhartha had been practicing with despised him and thought him worthless. "Let us go somewhere else to practice. He drinks milk, and he eats rice. He has no perseverance." But

Siddhartha did very well. Day in and day out he meditated, and developed his insight, his understanding, and his compassion very, very quickly as he recovered his health.[2]

Like the Buddha, all of us have grown up in a patriarchal culture. The religious authorities we encounter very likely resemble ascetic guardians of orthodox customs in their distrust of the body and the feminine. Milk is an archetypal symbol of feminine nourishment. Hence, the Buddha's act of drinking milk is a beautiful gesture of reconciliation with the feminine principle. Outwardly, he accepts a woman's nurturing care while inwardly his former harshness and severity soften into compassion for his body.

Like the Buddha, we are challenged to become our own teachers. Our path is like a subtle, exquisite dance; no set of instructions can replace our own intuitive artistry. When we surpass external rules, claiming our own authority, life becomes tremendously exciting. Each step has meaning, and there is no place for guilt—only for courageous learning through trial and error.

Following the Leader

For many Westerners, the idea of handing over responsibility for one's spiritual path to another person holds a powerful attraction. When we encounter living masters of any traditional religion, we may find the clarity and certainty of their beliefs very compelling compared to our own confused meanderings. We may yearn for the spiritual training they received, and be enchanted by the dignity and elegance of their ancient customs. But we should also consider the value of our own position as twentieth-century Westerners. Lacking a strong, living religious tradition of our own, we are free of the fetters of religious dogma. Instead of hurrying to adopt someone else's traditions, can we bear to live in the openness of not belonging?

The human psyche may now be standing on the threshold of its adulthood, with all the upheavals such a coming of age entails. As a result, our relationship to authority is necessarily changing as well. In earlier times, spiritual knowledge was transmitted through parent figures, wise elders to whom one surrendered in childlike obedience. Like actual parents, these spiritual teachers were not perfect and at times displayed their human failings. Even so, training under their tutelage provided the most effective means of absorbing spiritual knowledge. To this day in Asia, the path of the spiritual seeker is generally one of disciplehood. The teacher, as a living representative of an ancient tradition, is invested with complete authority, often assuming full responsibility for every aspect of the disciple's life.

At this time our challenge is to develop our own spiritual authority—to communicate with the spirit of guidance without intermediaries, and to recognize that spirit wherever we find it. Abdicating responsibility for our spiritual path and leaving it at the feet of another human being now represents a regressive movement that counteracts true growth. Today, any church based on a hierarchical power structure is no longer a viable vessel for spiritual authority.

The Authority of Form

If we choose to practice a traditional form of movement meditation, then we will need to respond mindfully and creatively to the form itself, remembering that the conventions that govern it and give each form its unique character were invented by human beings, and that these rules can always be questioned. The forms we use are merely vehicles of our learning process. A form is a sort of container, a language that allows us to communicate. It can be a tool for enlightenment, but it can also be a repressive device, stifling individuality and expressiveness. Dancer Gabrielle Roth speaks for many when she describes her experience of leaving dance classes feeling like a failure:

> Dance meant imitation, whether the form was ballet, modern, or James Brown funk. The focus was always on someone else's steps. . . . I left so many classes in despair, judging myself adversely for not being Martha Graham. Somehow, dance classes just kept proving to me that I wasn't good enough.[3]

A student who decides to study a non-Western tradition may find it necessary to adapt the established teachings to her own circumstances. All ethnic practices grew out of the soil of a specific time and place, in response to the immediate needs of the local people's unique mentality and circumstances. Such disciplines must be creatively adapted if they are to serve the needs of people in completely different cultural environments.

Obviously, this is a very delicate decision, since the sacred traditions of this planet's indigenous people are perhaps our most precious heritage. Whenever we alter them, there is always the danger that we might discard meaningful and essential elements that simply fall beyond our scope of comprehension. The discipline itself is sacred, and any decision to tamper with it ought to be made with great care.

At the same time, spiritual traditions have traveled from one culture to another throughout human history and in each case these traditions have been transformed. We therefore must not let reverence take our creative breath away; we have no other alternative than to go through the arduous process of reinventing teachings and breaking rules if we are to preserve the integrity of our practice. In the United States today, many spiritual seekers are creating their own brands of Hinduism, of Zen, of Shamanism, of Yoga, Aikido, and Tai Chi; and this is as it should be.

Meditation as the Practice of Presence

Why do we move our bodies when there is no need to move? Isn't it because something within us, some part of our soul, pushes outward and strives for expression? No movement is meaningful in and of itself. As a lamp needs to be lit from within, so movement must be illuminated by spiritual presence. The most sensual movement is lifeless unless it is an authentic expression of the mover's sensuality. But a very slight movement, when an authentic expression of a person's truth, carries profound meaning and spiritual power.

Meditation has been described as the *practice of presence*. Truth and presence are synonymous, for how can we know truth if we are not fully present in the moment? Movement meditation is the practice of maintaining presence or truthfulness while moving. The basic instruction for most of the meditations included here is simply to *move, breathe,* and *pay attention.* Everything else is extra. Since we move and breathe all day long, we have ample opportunity to practice.

Because so much of our suffering arises in relationship to thoughts about the past and the future, the practice of presence invites us to lay down the burden of memory and to delight in the perfection of the moment: the dark wood grain of a table, the smell of cinnamon, a cup of steaming coffee. All our movements can be sacred art, whether we are walking down the street or dancing in a temple.

Most of the time we move automatically, habitually. Preoccupied with goals, we do not notice *how* we move. But in movement meditation we set aside time to simply focus on the process of movement. We must be willing to maintain a state of unknowing, a state of witnessing movement without demanding to know its meaning or purpose. Let go of the need to control, and try to approach your movements with an attitude of curious but respectful witnessing. This very lack of purpose will give you the freedom to explore territory that lies outside your ordinary range of perception.

There are areas within our bodies to which we never pay attention, whole groups of muscles that we never use. As we begin to use these parts of our bodies, long-forgotten thoughts and emotions may surface. The body is in fact a vessel, a storehouse of your entire history: everything you ever experienced has left traces.

Knowledge we acquire through precise observation of our own movements liberates us in a very practical way. People tend to be very casual about self-observation. For example, we may be aware that we get angry in certain situations, but we may not recognize just *how* we manifest our anger. Unless we realize that we clench our jaws, or hold our breath, or tighten our backs, we do not have the choice to change our behavior. We are stuck in habitual reactions. Once we know exactly what we do, we have options. Instead of tensing, we can choose to take a deep breath and relax. In this way, moment-by-moment awareness builds a bridge from rigidity to fluidity.

From Awkwardness to Grace

If you feel awkward, movement meditation is a wonderful discipline for you because it offers the opportunity to overcome this negative self-image and discover the joy of living in your body. Most people I work with are not dancers; many were initially terrified of just about any kind of movement. But in movement meditation, there is no single correct way of moving and no place for competitiveness. In fact, it may be easier for a non-dancer to experience the "beginner's mind," so essential to movement meditation, than for an experienced dancer who takes for granted the mystery of simple movement.

Part of overcoming awkwardness lies in understanding its sources. People are not generally born clumsy—they become that way. Awkwardness often masks the very real pain of not feeling entirely safe and at home in the physical world. If you feel awkward or painfully self-conscious, you may want to think or write about the following questions:

In what ways are you afraid of being seen, and where do the roots of this fear lie? Ironically, being fully seen is what we most long for, and yet what we most avoid. How can we feel loved unless we let down our masks and allow ourselves to be seen for who we truly are? Yet to be visible also means to be vulnerable and open to rejection.

What messages did you receive about your body and your appearance, both during childhood and afterward? Children are often made to feel uncomfortable and awkward about themselves. Because children are so sensitive to the approval or disapproval of adults, a single negative judgment can become a painful belief harbored for an entire lifetime.

Are there other ways in which your self-esteem was undermined? A child who is told that he is stupid may not only begin to act as if he really were dull-minded, but also to move awkwardly and without confidence. There are so many ways—both subtle and direct—of letting a child know that he is deficient: many children who are well cared for materially are inwardly starved for affection, tenderness, and acceptance. A child who feels unloved will assume he is unlovable, because children almost inevitably blame themselves, not their parents, for lack of nurturing. Even positive judgments can be subtle traps: a little girl who always hears how pretty she looks may feel pressured to appear pretty all the time, even though at times she would far rather be wild, dirty, or angry. We reflect all these self-concepts in our body structure and the way we move. Our bodies are literally molded by our beliefs and self-images. Shedding old beliefs can often cause dramatic changes in the physical body itself.

Are there ways in which you unconsciously benefit from your awkwardness or use it to protect yourself? A common belief is, "If I were attractive and powerful, I would get into trouble. I would have to deal with people's attraction to me as well as with their jealousy and aggression." Many people need to learn that it is possible to be attractive—especially sexually attractive—successful, and powerful, and at the same time safe. We need to find supportive and respectful friends who encourage our success and enjoy the company of powerful peers.

Consider the issue of authority once again. Ask yourself, to which people and to what internal voices you give up your own authority? How would you move and act differently, if you were truly to claim your personal authority?

Moving with Love

As the heart opens to love, the entire body is set aglow. The acclaimed cancer surgeon Dr. Bernie Siegel emphasizes the healing power of love and emotional expressiveness. People who communicate deeply and intimately, Siegel writes, have been proven less likely to develop serious diseases; their immune systems and their self-healing abilities are stronger than average. Working out at the gym or in aerobics classes may strengthen your heart physiologically, but it will not give you the inner radiance or the real foundation for a healthy life that comes from moving in a sacred way. Sacred movement should help you fall in love with life and kindle the light of love in your body.

How can we feel love for ourselves or for others if we are ashamed of our bodies and who we are? Meditation allows you to become familiar with your inner judge and to disengage from criticism. If you are aware of the judging voices and still believe that they speak the truth, you have not examined them deeply enough. Question their assumptions and their logic more carefully. A voice that asserts you are in any way undeserving of love is never a truthful voice, no matter how rationally convincing it may sound.

Group Work

All the meditations taught in this book can be adapted to a group situation. Practicing with a supportive circle of people offers great benefits. A group acts as a vortex, exponentially amplifying the energies present; a group of only a dozen people can create an extremely powerful field of energy that, especially during trance work, is an enormous benefit. People will effortlessly enter altered states of consciousness within the circle and will feel safer in doing so than they would on their own.

The dynamics of group work are complex and I will comment only very briefly on them in this context. An important consideration in establishing a group is to create a nonjudgmental, secure atmosphere. Performance anxiety is very deeply rooted in our society. It is a symptom of our distrust and repression of the body and results from the fact that people are no longer used to dancing together as a community. Anxiety arises when we realize that our body is on display, that we may be looked at and judged, and that there is nothing our mind can do to control the situation.

On the other hand, the experience of being the center of attention in a supportive, nonjudgmental atmosphere can be exhilarating and profoundly healing. When young children dance, they love to receive attention. Animals, birds, and fish dance in order to attract and woo their mates, displaying an awesome array of bodily ornaments such as vibrant markings and colorful feathers, all of which underscore their dances. There is a natural element of exhibitionism in dance; to dance is to make a display. Consciously or unconsciously, the dancer shows off her body; indeed, the body demands to be noticed, observed, and appreciated. In order to transform self-consciousness and fear into confidence, people need to have a positive experience of being seen with love and compassion, receiving attention without being judged.

As we learn to move and behave in new ways that initially feel intimidating, we must do so in a social environment that is supportive; otherwise we simply run the risk of being wounded once again. Circles amplify whatever energies are present within them. If fear and judgment are present, and are not acknowledged and worked through, they will destroy the circle. But a circle, as long as it remains unobstructed by fear, amplifies love. Just as a healthy animal instinctively moves toward its needs, so also the circle is inherently attracted to love. A conscious group leader will support this tendency and deal with blockages as they arise.

When people dare to move, speak, and act with openness, love, and mutual acceptance, they create an enormously powerful vessel of transformation. Sharing our journey with others, we find that we confront the same fears, the same needs, obsessions, and feelings. There is absolutely no inner state that others have not also experienced. Inevitably, one person's process will free another, or help him to break through in his own inner work. Those who on their own would succumb to fear may with group support gain the courage to enter the fire and allow their own transformation. They know that they can rely on the circle to support them and help them work through whatever emotional or mental issues that surface. The strength and validation that blossom forth in an environment of trust and intimacy is immeasurable.

Because love is contagious, every step you take toward love is a step toward the healing of your family and the planet, as well as your own healing. As Thich Nhat Hanh observes, we can create peace only by "being peace."

Getting Ready

To begin the practice of movement meditation on your own, all you need is your body and a private, undisturbed place. In the beginning, the sense of being safe in your space is crucial. You may find yourself moving in some very strange ways and making some very strange sounds. Like prayer, movement meditation is a very personal, intimate process and should be respected as such.

At the end of this book you will find a list of suggested music for movement meditation. Music is an invaluable tool, and I recommend that you prepare some tapes that you enjoy and that inspire you to move.

Some meditations involve sitting. In movement meditation, the most important part of the body is your spine; you can spend hours doing movement meditation in a sitting position. Give some thought to finding a form of sitting that works for you. If you find it impossible to sit comfortably for any extended period of time, find an alternative position. For instance, you can train yourself to lie on your back without falling asleep. Without a good sitting posture, however, it is difficult to let yourself drop deeply into inner space. So, it is really worthwhile trying to develop a good sitting posture, one in which your spine is upright and balanced.

Don't try to sit cross-legged if you know you can only stand it for ten minutes. It is fine to sit on a chair, provided you can put your bare feet flat on the ground. Another good way of sitting is on a Zen bench, a very low, sloped bench that you tuck under your buttocks after kneeling on the ground. You may need to practice some stretches and gradually build up the strength in your back by first sitting for just two or three minutes, and gradually lengthening the period. After the body has had a chance to balance itself energetically through movement, it settles into the sitting posture far more easily, without much resistance or restlessness. Many people like myself who previously found it impossible to sit in meditation for any length of time eventually learn to sit quite easily.

As I mentioned previously, anyone can practice movement meditation. If you are physically challenged or must use a wheelchair, movement meditation can allow you to be fully in touch with your body and sometimes even expand the range of your abilities beyond limitations you previously accepted. The key once again lies in claiming your authority and taking full responsibility for yourself. Be willing to play, gently stretching to explore the edges of your body and mind, and learn to give full, undivided attention to your movements. Among the meditations are several which are suitable or can be adapted to almost any physical problem. Use them, and create your own!

Consult your physician if you have any questions about your ability to practice the more physically challenging exercises. Never do anything physically painful or push your body beyond its limits. Beware of any voice that tells you you are inadequate, that you need to be more creative, beautiful, flexible, or any other quality. Such beliefs will prevent you from accepting yourself as you are in this moment, and may cause unnecessary injuries. When there is no attachment to a certain identity, no holding on to moving in a certain way, we are free—we can allow ourselves to be anything we want, even foolish, clumsy, silly, ridiculous, or ugly. We can accept that the truth of who you are changes moment by moment.

Each chapter in this book deals with a particular way by which the life-force moves through us, from the subtle rhythms of the heartbeat to the most extroverted forms of dance. The meditations need not be done in the order they appear. Remember that they are merely starting points, intended to inspire you to explore your interior world. Once you take the first step, your own body will guide you. All the meditations are interrelated, so you can start at any point that interests you. They can generally be practiced after reading the instructions one or more times. If you decide to read them aloud and record them, however, make sure you leave plenty of time between paragraphs for your own inner experience. If you practice with a friend or in a group, people may take turns guiding.

Discipline

Movement meditation complements most other forms of spiritual practice. I encourage people to work with a wide variety of methods such as body-work, art, therapy, Tarot, dream work, visualizations, and writing. But regardless of what type of spiritual practice we choose, discipline is essential; without deep commitment to the process of our unfolding, we get stuck in the ruts of our ego. Discipline, in the spiritual sense, is not punishment or repression; the word comes from the Latin *discere,* "to learn": discipline is the path through which we learn the knowledge of liberation.

People sometimes ask me why I approach dancing as a spiritual discipline. My answer is quite simple: I love to dance; it is one of the things in life for which I feel true passion. There is no reason why gardening, or building kites, or breeding ocelots can't be your spiritual practice, provided you pursue it with an enduring passion. Eventually we can learn to do everything in a mindful way. Until then, we need to start practicing somewhere. It is also true that whatever moves you deeply is also bound to bring deep feelings of resistance. So keep going: if your knee is injured, don't strain it, choose a sitting movement meditation. If your room is tiny, learn to dance in small spaces.

Discipline takes a different form for everyone. Ultimately, discipline is an inner attitude of dedication to the process of unfolding and to the realization of truth. The effects of movement meditation, as with any other form of spiritual practice, radiate out from our discipline into daily life to increase our awareness of what is really happening moment by moment, and to increase our ability to remain centered and open in the midst of activities. The real discipline, the grand discipline, is your life. Everything else is just practice, sowing seeds.

CHAPTER THREE

Moving into Stillness

Ten thousand flowers in spring, the moon in autumn,
a cool breeze in summer, snow in winter.
If your mind isn't clouded by unnecessary things,
this is the best season of your life.

      WU-MEN

Empty yourself of everything.
Let the mind rest at peace.
The ten thousand things rise and fall while the Self watches their
   return.

      LAO TSU

The stillness in stillness is not the real stillness. Only when there is stillness in movement can the spiritual rhythm appear which pervades heaven and earth.

      TS'AI-KEN T'AN

Approaching Stillness

IMAGINE: at the break of dawn, you are floating in a small boat over the waters of a pristine lake. No wind, no ripple ruffles the mirror-smooth surface. Glancing down, you see the luminous sky reflected in perfect clarity. Such is the state of a still, peaceful heart, which effortlessly contains and reflects the vastness of spiritual truth.

Deep meditation offers a path into inner silence; yet, no amount of will power can force the mind to fall silent. On the contrary, the more you try to control it, the less you succeed. The mind by its very nature is a thought-producing factory, and like all organs it has an innate need to perform its function. There is no sense fighting it. Instead, simply let it be and try to remain present in your body, present with your breath. Your thoughts continue to race through time and space. But if you can resist the temptation to fuel them with your attention, they will gradually begin to slow down.

Traditional sitting meditation calls for bodily stillness as a means of encouraging inner silence. Yet merely suppressing movement is usually not helpful; in suppressing it, the impulse to move transforms into mental activity and physical tension. These forms of sitting meditation were designed for people who did not live in an urban environment, their days spent in offices or at computers, which tend to create a state of imbalance between head and body. If you have concentrated all your energy in the head, you should bring your center of awareness back down into the body before sitting. Otherwise you will needlessly struggle with an excess of mental activity.

Meditative movement allows excess mental energy to be transformed into physical energy. It represents the perfect complement to sitting meditation by balancing your physical and mental energy so you avoid getting entangled in needless inner struggle.

In terms of energy, the belly and the heart are the most radiant parts of the body. Because of this, an easy way of shifting from mental involvement into bodily presence is to bring your attention either to your belly or your heart. Experiment with this right now. Become aware of the present moment and of your breath, and lay one hand on your heart to help you center your attention there. Automatically, the mind begins to release tension and fear, relaxing into the spaciousness of the present, and absorbing the qualities of compassion and gentleness.

So begins the process of emptying, the process of coming down to earth and settling into what is simple and essential: the soft belly, the peaceful heart. In theory, this sounds very wonderful and soothing. The problem is that, while we might think we want peace, this is rarely true. We generally prefer to be entertained over being peaceful. When we seek out emptiness, we soon realize how attached we are to projects, ideas, possessions, experiences, concepts—and how very uncomfortable emptiness is. We need to be patient with our mind and realize that, just as the stomach is conditioned to demand food, the mind is conditioned to gather information: the mind by its very nature resists emptiness.

Accustomed to entertainment, we crave constant input. If deprived of stimulation, our mind responds with symptoms of withdrawal—restlessness, anxiety, and boredom. Boredom is to the mind what hunger is to the body. Just as fasting sometimes will serve as a healing tool, similarly enduring boredom can be a valuable ingredient of spiritual practice. When you feel bored, this indicates that your mind is running out of fuel and has not yet surrendered into the richness of the present moment. Be more fully present, and you will no longer be bored.

In any form of spiritual practice we must be willing to face boredom, recognizing it as one of the guardians at the threshold of emptiness. But in movement meditation, the willingness to face boredom is especially important because the body tends to learn at a slower pace than the mind. Most people get bored with a new movement and give up practicing it long before their body has had a chance to fully incorporate the new information. When you find a movement you would like to explore, practice it not only once but many times. Only then is there a possibility of embodying it fully and of dropping to a deeper, more subtle level of experience. Through practicing any movement meditatively, you can reach the stage of perfection that is marked by effortlessness, grace, and unhurried presence. Never think that because you can easily execute a movement you know it. Certain simple movements contain great power that can only be acquired by humbly and persistently meditating on them. These movements I call *movement mantras;* through repetition, the wisdom embodied in them enters your body and psyche and continues to unfold at increasingly deeper levels.

Contrast

Let us briefly consider three of the tools we possess that deepen our connection with stillness: contrast, inner listening, and completion.

Consider contrast. When you emerge from a darkened room, the brightness of light blinds the eyes. After passing a few moments of intense pain, you appreciate the sensations of pleasure and well-being all the more. Likewise, if you tighten a taut muscle even further before releasing it, the muscle will become aware of the contrast and understand: this is tension; this is release. In this way, contrast heightens awareness.

Sometimes the fastest way to reach a goal is to travel in the opposite direction. Next time you find yourself obsessed with a concern, your mind tangled up in worry, try turning on some wild dance music—music that really makes your body want to move, music with a drive. Turn up the volume as much as your environment permits, and invite every part of your body to move. Don't dance as you might in an elegant nightclub. Let go of your self-image as a doctor, parent, respectable person, and allow your wilder, more primitive animal-spirit to emerge. Imagine yourself somewhere where hot, sweaty bodies are fine. And as you dance, make noises: singing, grunting, howling. Give way to whatever your body suggests. Exaggerate. Roll on the floor and let out the crazy person hidden within the sane one. Move shamelessly, outrageously.

Then, stop abruptly and turn off the music. Lie down and watch your breath as it quiets down. After such a tempest of sound and motion, silence refreshes like a fountain of water. Relish the serenity of *non-doing,* of simply resting in your being.

In retrospect, I realize that my teenage love affair with dance clubs had a lot to do with the thrill I felt every time I walked from the blasting music into the silent night. The experience of radical contrast can increase our awareness of the unchanging witness within. Extreme contrasts have the power to jolt the sleeping soul into wide-awake attention, which is why they play such an important role in traditional initiation rites. To the extent that one identifies oneself as a person in pain or a person in ecstasy, the experience of contrast turns one's self-definition inside out, and yet there is someone who has passed *through* the contrasts, witnessing them impassively. This recognition, this spark of wonderment, is the beginning of autonomy, which comes to fruition when an individual can keep her calm in the midst of outer turbulence, can stay balanced among unbalanced people. Then, the urban jungle points the way to the calm of the inner oasis, and frantic, hectic energy becomes a reminder to slow down and breathe. When the outer environment is nourishing and supportive, one merges with it, but when it is hostile and negative, one maintains balance by establishing a positive, peaceful energy field within.

Once I led a movement medicine circle in a hall near a very busy street corner, the favorite hangout of all the local kids. Inside, we would dance and drum our way into deep states of inner silence. All the while, the sound of sirens and of yelling, laughing, and fighting men would drift into the windows. Eventually we discovered we could either become irritated and resentful at the intrusion, or we could make use of the contrast to carry us into an even deeper space of silence. At times, despite the commotion on the street, the sense of peace within the room was almost palpable.

Inner Listening

Indian mythology holds that once, when walking through the forest, the Hindu god Rama heard someone call his name. None of his companions could hear anything, for their ability to listen was not as refined as the god's. But he could hear a female voice calling him faintly, but distinctly, "Rama! Rama!" He followed the sound until he came to a boulder from which the cry seemed to be emerging. Gently Rama laid his hands upon it. The minute he touched the rock, it began to move and dissolve and transform. Finally a beautiful woman stood before him. Her name was Ahalya; a curse had imprisoned her within stone until touched by the god himself. She had been there for eons, crying out his name in a voice that only he could hear.

Ahalya's story is our own story. Parts of us are petrified and locked away within the depths of our body, and unless we learn to listen carefully and compassionately, we will never hear their urgent call. Thus, *listening* describes the basic attitude with which we try to enter into relationship with ourselves and others. Try thinking of the heart as the organ of inner listening. By listening with the heart, we develop understanding and compassion for ourselves, and we learn to replenish our interior space with consciousness and light. Listening is the basis of all healing.

As you read, pause a moment to listen to the sounds around you. As I write these pages, I too, am listening. I hear the patter of rain on window, the sound of a wind chime, the distant roar of an airplane. Earlier, we spoke of shifting from the mind to the heart or belly. Let me add another way of coming into presence: you can shift from thinking to listening. Listen to your breath for a moment, to its even rhythm. As you listen into your body, you may perceive many things that have no audible sound: an old familiar pain in the right knee, a twinge in the neck, a warmth around the solar plexus. Receptivity to inner movement is an essential ingredient of movement meditation. Listening to the body takes a special kind of concentration that many people never develop; even dancers are rarely trained to listen to their bodies.

Humans have placed radar systems like giant ears upon the surface of the earth to listen into outer space and scan the emptiness for faint signals. Our body is a microcosm of this universe, equally unknown and vast, full of darkness and light, sound and silence, mingling in intricate swirling dances. Though we perceive our body as solid, it is actually shockingly empty, each molecule surrounded by as much empty space proportionately as is each planet in our solar system. Like the Buddhist void that gives birth to all forms, this inner emptiness is charged with the potent force of creative consciousness.

To explore these inner regions, working with contrast is not sufficient. Contrast can awaken the sleeping psyche and remind us of the healing power of silence. But having entered into wakefulness, how long can we maintain it? We may find that almost imperceptibly we lapse into forgetfulness of the present moment as our attention shifts from the heart and

Northwest Coast Native American totem
pole representing the birth of the universe
from the void.

belly back to the restless mind. So in addition to working with contrast, we
must cultivate inner listening.

Try rocking or swaying very gently. Notice what happens. Notice how
the movement engenders a slight friction in parts of your body, like an inward massage. When a masseuse lays her hands on a tight muscle, she
brings awareness back into the forgotten muscles and reminds them of their
ability to release; thus she quite literally helps the person re-member. Conscious movement does the same thing from within, bringing consciousness
into forgotten places within the body. Through listening, we begin the process of inner housecleaning, of releasing old patterns and discovering the
option of simplicity. Our life, inner and outer, becomes more spacious and
our movements more basic.

It is quite unnecessary and indeed impossible to know what you will be
doing a year, or even an hour from now. But if you listen closely enough,
you will find that out of this moment, your next movement emerges with
absolute clarity. Just as water wants to flow in a certain direction, so your
own life has a direction, of which your conscious mind may be completely
unaware. When you practice walking meditation, listen carefully and you

will find that every step carries within it the seed of the next. Walk very slowly, and you discover that your feet know exactly where they want to place themselves. Even swerving one inch this way or that may disturb the harmony of the flow. By listening into your own movements, you will discover that each situation, each posture carries within itself its own resolution. No situation is unworkable.

Completion

Sometimes even listening is not enough. The psyche contains certain powerful complexes of thoughts and emotions that cannot be transformed or dissolved by merely listening to them and observing them dispassionately. Rather, they demand some form of external completion through interactions that take place in the outer world.

The Indian spiritual teacher Paramahansa Yogananda tells an interesting story about the enlightened master Mahiri Lahasaya.[1] Near the end of his training, Mahiri Lahasaya was taken into the Himalayas, where he met the great saint Babaji. In the midst of the wilderness Babaji created a fantastic golden palace for Mahiri Lahasaya, resplendent with gems and exquisite art. Mahiri Lahasaya realized that he had always longed for such opulent beauty. Running his hands along the jewel-studded walls, his mind was flooded with a profound sense of fulfillment and release. Babaji then explained that this hidden desire had presented the only obstacle to Mahiri Lahasaya's enlightenment—and that Babaji had created the entire palace just so that this last desire could be consummated and set aside.

It is interesting to encounter this story in the context of a religious philosophy otherwise so dedicated to renunciation of desire. Even here it is acknowledged that certain ego states cannot be overcome through detachment and meditation alone. Mahiri Lahasaya's psyche insisted that his fantasy be enacted in the outer world. Most therapists also realize that certain mind-states must be entered into and completed before the emotional charge can be released. Certain feelings must be expressed, certain words spoken, certain energies allowed to flow outwardly.

Regrettably, meditation has often been misused as a means of escape into an introverted state. Solitary practice should ideally be combined with some form of relationship practice, and sitting with moving forms of meditation. Alone, we may quite successfully keep painful or frightening feelings walled in. Because our unhealed psychic wounds tend to stem from negative experiences in human relations, we can easily fool ourselves into believing we are fine as long as we withdraw. Our problems do not disappear, however; they merely lie dormant like a cold snake. When the right trigger is released, they spring into action. We have a fight, or someone rejects us, and suddenly we become inordinately upset, depressed, or angry.

Sometimes it is appropriate to surrender to grief and to identify fully with the frightened, lonely child inside ourselves. Then, it is essential that we have the humility to allow ourselves to sob, to beat on a pillow, to throw a tantrum and scream, instead of habitually containing our emotions. Here, movement affords a very natural and gentle way of allowing emotions to emerge and be expressed and transformed, thus representing a powerful therapeutic tool.

At other times becoming engaged with our emotional states may be mere self-indulgence. In these instances, we need to quietly observe the fearful thoughts or the painful ones without encouraging our inner involvement or identification. To discriminate between these situations is not easy; no technique can substitute for awareness and honesty. Each situation is new and different, and we must look carefully and listen so that we can choose the next step with awareness rather than out of habit. Inner work is art, and in art there are no absolute rules.

Emptiness

Emptiness is both healing and humbling—healing because it puts our worries into perspective, humbling because it reveals our smallness in the universe. Outer emptiness helps us contact that within us which is equally empty, open, and unlimited. The lonely places, the silent places, the desolate places, can help us come face to face with our god. Against a backdrop of silence, movement emerges out of a deep blue infinity and melts back into it, each gesture radiant and luminous. These movements are no longer "ours" in a personal way: we watch them, aware of the realm of silence just behind them. Thoughts slow down, and at times there is just this watching, this listening. As Peter Matthiessen notes:

> Like the round-bottomed Bodhidharma doll, returning to its center, meditation represents the foundation of the universe, to which all returns, as in the stillness of the dead of night, the stillness between tides and winds, the stillness of the instant before Creation.[2]

Emptiness and fullness are yin and yang: they are lovers, and must be in balance. Because our mind is biased in favor of fullness, the full and the empty spaces in our life have fallen out of balance. Spiritual seekers have always been drawn to retreats and monasteries, spaces where one could lead a radically simplified life, an existence of solitude, stillness, and emptiness. In today's industrial societies, many people find that their life is too full—too full of things to do, of worries, too full of traffic and noise and congestion. Fear of emptiness causes us to make life immensely more complicated, cluttering life with all kinds of excess baggage, both physical and mental. The more we accumulate, the more overwhelming life becomes. We begin to long for simplicity and quiet. For most of us, the challenge is to live a life of simplicity without withdrawing from society.

Our present way of life, one in which many people have begun to appreciate the value of emptiness, is probably new in the history of humankind. For millennia, human beings have been plagued by boredom. Long stretches of time passed during which cattle grazed, seasons came and went, and only rarely did something truly extraordinary occur. Humans valued excitement, not emptiness. Now that our world has become so full of complexity, however, we appreciate silence and emptiness. In discovering the healing power of silence in the outer world, we also awaken to the value of inner silence. For constant activity, stimulation, and worry crush the light of our spirit.

To rebalance ourselves, we must consciously search out empty places. Spend some time in the desert or by the ocean. Lie down on a hillside and gaze into the sky, or into the infinity of a starlit night. Create an empty, uncluttered, yet beautiful space in your home—a room with white walls, a simple seat, and perhaps a flower, or a candle. Dare to spend more time alone, granting yourself moments of nothingness—of sitting quietly, breathing, just being. Such spaces of simplicity and non-doing are healing medicine. In the same way, the most healing movements are empty ones, free of intention and purpose. Like the wind, like the falling of snowflakes, they simply are. We need open spaces inside us. We should take care not to obliterate such spaces, for they are like the stained glass windows in a cathedral, letting in the sunlight. In *The Solace of Open Spaces,* Gretel Ehrlich, contemplating the expanses of Wyoming, wrote:

> Space has a spiritual equivalent and can heal what is divided and burdensome in us. My grandchildren will probably use space shuttles for a honeymoon trip or to recover from heart attacks, but closer to home we might also learn how to carry space inside ourselves in the effortless way we carry our skins. Space represents sanity, not a life purified, dull or "spaced out" but one that might accommodate intelligently any idea or situation.
>
> From the clayey soil of northern Wyoming is mined bentonite, which is used as a filler in candy, gum, and lipstick. We Americans are great on fillers, as if what we have, what we are, is not enough. We have a cultural tendency toward denial, but, being affluent, we strangle ourselves with what we can buy. We have only to look at the houses we build to see how we build *against* space, the way we drink against pain and loneliness. We fill up space as if it were a pie shell, with things whose opacity further obstructs our ability to see what is already there.[3]

Using Death as a Teacher

Whenever a void appears, fear begins to arise, and regardless of whether we are sitting still or moving, we may find ourselves bolting. We run away, escaping into errands or other distractions as we approach the threshold of true stillness. We have all acquired techniques of manipulating our environment. But inner emptiness is unknowable and beyond our control. Like outer space, it has no up or down, no right or wrong. It reminds us unpleasantly of death—and indeed, emptiness is death to the ego, for if we allow it to expand, the ego is annihilated. Spiritual practice challenges us to "die" moment by moment until all selfhood is totally dissolved in enlightenment: "I saw my own death with my own eyes," sings an Indian saint in one of his songs of ecstasy.

More than any other form of spiritual practice, meditation on the body confronts us with our own impermanence. Rather than dwelling intellectually on death as a distant future event, it is essential to delve into the physical experience of our own dying as an ongoing process in every moment of our lives. Without confronting death, real spiritual progress cannot occur. Disconnected from the body, it is relatively easy to enter states of bliss or ecstasy, but such experiences have little value in themselves. It is essential to fully acknowledge all the emotions that arise as we contemplate our mortality—the fear of suffering and death, as well as the love and compassion we feel for the short-lived but beautiful flower of the body.

Movement meditation is a branch of *Tantric* practice, which means that we do not cut ourselves off from our body, despite its vulnerability, nor do we repress sexual energy, despite the haunting proximity of sexuality and death. Orgasm has sometimes been called the "little death" because of the surrender of separateness and self-control involved. Moreover, conception—the biological outcome of sexuality—brings us face to face with the fact that we are not immortal but are destined to surrender our life-force to the next generation. In counseling women, I have often noted the deep association between sexual experience and the very immediate and profound encounter with death involved in childbirth.

When we look death in the face, it forces us to reevaluate our entire life. In Bernie Siegel's stories of his work with cancer patients, we see how tragic and at the same time immensely joyful facing death can be, as patients realize, often for the first time in their life, that their life really is their own, theirs to do with as they please. In such a situation, the insanity of allowing fear to dictate one's moves and the wisdom of opening the heart and "following one's bliss," as Joseph Campbell put it, become apparent.

It requires great courage to fully accept our humanity. There is so much vulnerability, grief, and sadness, both in ourselves and in the world; everything feels so raw when one begins to live with an open heart. If we decide to allow ourselves to feel this pain anyway, it is because we realize that to live in fear is to live in the shadow of death. Embracing our humanity is a choice of life over death, and paradoxically we often require a heightened awareness of impending physical death before we can muster the courage to choose life.

Our society, in its attempt to conquer death, has encapsulated the natural process of dying in a shell of technology, segregating the dying from the living. The dying are surrounded by life-support systems, numbed with drugs, and secluded in sterilized environments. We want the benevolent face of nature without the terrifying one. In the process of avoiding death, we have surrounded it with barriers of fear and denial. In one of his letters, the German poet Rainer Maria Rilke wrote:

> I reproach all modern religions for having provided their believers with consolations and glossings-over of death, instead of giving them the means of coming to an understanding with it. With it and with its full, unmasked cruelty: this cruelty is so immense that it is precisely with *it* that the circle closes; it leads back into a mildness which is greater, purer, and more perfectly clear (all consolation is muddy!) than we have ever, even on the sweetest spring day, imagined mildness to be.[4]

Instead of denying the reality of death and dying, we should meditate upon them as the teachers they are. They remind us that the time to live and love is now. When we accept death not as cause for fear, but simply as a given fact, we honor the preciousness of everyone we meet. We realize we may never see this person again, and this awareness encourages us to express our feelings openly without procrastinating. When we remember death, we become aware of the value of each moment of life. As Thich Nhat Hanh says, "Dwelling in the present moment I know this is the only moment."[5] When are you going to live, if not now?

Simplicity

As people move through their process of spiritual and psychic healing, they often speak of a new sense of simplicity, spaciousness, and unclutteredness. They may go through closets and give away piles of old possessions, or give up old acquaintances, or old habits. Above all, a new spaciousness unfolds within. A clarity emerges, which refreshes and liberates.

The principles of simplicity and effortlessness are essential to movement meditation and to spiritual life in general. The greatest obstacle to conscious movement is not being unable to perform a certain movement, but rather being unable to prevent superfluous movements. A single hand gesture, coming out of inner stillness, can have profound power and meaning. All the sacred arts, in fact, have their roots within the unlimited, ever-present space Buddhists call the void.

Whenever you watch a true dancer, you will see this absolute simplicity and sparsity. Watching such artists, onlookers say "It looks so easy." You find the same simple beauty of movement in highly evolved spiritual teachers; such simplicity requires discipline. It requires that we be willing to carefully examine where our real priorities lie, and to ponder the attachments that chain us to patterns of unnecessary activity. Simplicity is truly easy, yet such ease is won through great discipline—and maintaining the discipline can be difficult.

When a truly great dancer moves, every movement is essential. Like a Rilke poem or a classic haiku, nothing extra remains to be stripped away. The many movements we perform for the sake of ego leave us feeling exhausted and depleted. Those born of stillness, on the other hand, draw forth our inner power. Through movement meditation, you will learn to recognize essential movements. Rising from the void, they have no obvious purpose, yet, like the flight of a heron through the mist, they are precise and charged with mystery.

CHAPTER THREE: MEDITATIONS

Rattling the Bones

RECOMMENDED MUSIC: For this meditation you will need a long piece of music with a steady rhythmic beat. I recommend *Gateway to the Sun,* which has a monotonous drumbeat accompanied by rattles with hardly any variation from beginning to end, or *Journey of the Drums* (see *Recommended Music,* page 240).

Rattling the bones is an extremely important practice. The Shakers used it, as do many Native American groups and African tribes. Many of us today are forced to face and process a great deal of fear, and shaking is a powerful antidote to fear. If you are struggling with anxiety attacks and fear, practice this meditation for fifteen minutes daily. Shaking also helps adjust and re-align the vertebrae, and allows tension held in the body's joints to release. It is one of the simplest and most effective ways of emptying the mind, grounding, and entering a light trance, and an excellent preparation for sitting meditation.

Stand and plant your feet firmly on the earth. Close your eyes.

Can you feel the vertical line that runs from the sky all the way down through your spine, right into the earth's center?

As the music begins, this axis begins to vibrate with the beat, shaking up and down. At first, there should be no side to side movement, just an up and down shaking.

Feel this shaking; let it enter your mind and body. Your legs and especially your knees should be soft and bouncy like springs, so that your spine can move.

Many people make the mistake of holding their necks rigidly, as if they fear their head might fall off. But no, it won't. You may lose your mind, but you won't lose your head. Try letting your neck soften just a little. Imagine having a child's head again, completely soft, free, and unbound.

Open yourself to the sound of the music and feel the heaven-earth axis vibrating. Let its rhythm take over and move you, until you find that the rhythm itself shakes you, vibrates you.

As you shake, empty out your mind. Shake out the thoughts as they arise. Shake out the comments, the expectations, the criticisms, the plans, the memories. . . .

Until there is nothing left but this vertical axis from heaven to earth, like a lightning rod, and along this axis, a steady shaking rhythm.

Your body dissolves, disintegrates, its solidity shaken apart. Belly shaking, heart shaking, shoulders shaking loose, all the muscles dissolving into vibration. Head is shaking, skull is shaking, neck is shaking. Vibration shaking out of your fingertips. Nothing remains but the rhythm that shakes you.

Listen to the rattle—take its sound into your body. Your body is the rattle, now. Feel the empty spaces within you, and in these spaces the rattling. Unless you empty yourself, there can be no rattling. So shake free some space inside for the rattling.

Breathe, and surrender to the shaking. Keep it easy. Feel that you could do this for hours without tiring. No pushing. Surrender to it. Shake your joints free until you feel as loose as a rag doll.

Continue shaking for at least fifteen to twenty minutes. Then stop abruptly. Sit or lie down.

Breathe. Move into silence, and let the silence receive and envelop your being.

Notice that, within you, something has been watching this entire process.

Something is aware of your breath as it comes in, and something is aware of your breath as it flows out.

There is a listener within you. There is an attentiveness. There is someone who perceives you fully and accepts you with compassion. A part of you is very wide and spacious and free, like a great hand into which you can lay yourself.

As soon as you try to grab hold of this something, it is gone. It vanishes, and there is nothing there at all. The minute you try to catch it, it evaporates.

Give yourself permission not to figure anything out, not to understand, to be an idiot. Give your brain permission to be just another body part, no more.

Let it relax and enjoy its connection with all the other body parts: heart, belly, genitals, feet. They are all important, too. Breathe nourishing light through every part of you.

If your body wants to move, let it move. Stillness is not something different, something separate from movement. There is a great silence, a great stillness within. Not the opposite of sound, not the opposite of the shaking, but underneath it.

Listen. Listen to the flow of your breath, to the flow of your thoughts. And sense the stillness just underneath. No need to silence them, but watch as they float upon silence like leaves on a wide river.

Listen, not with your mind, but with your being. Just listening. Listening to the space around your body . . . Listening to the sounds . . . Letting the sounds float through the silence like snowflakes drifting earthward.

Sit as long as you want, allow stillness to permeate your body and mind, and move more deeply into the stillness with each breath.

Inner Peace Meditation

RECOMMENDED MUSIC: Meditation music

This visualization is best used when you already are in a quiet, calm state of mind and want to move into a deeper stillness. In my groups, I would do this meditation only after we have done some dancing and people are warm, relaxed, and ready to settle down and go inward.

The beautiful story of Jesus on the lake, from Luke 8: 22–5, reminds us that what is within is also without; he who has perfect peace in his heart can also calm the stormy waters of the sea:

One day, he got into a boat with his disciples and said to them, "Let us cross over to the other side of the lake." So they put to sea, and as they sailed he fell asleep. When a squall came down on the lake the boat started taking in water and they found themselves in danger. So they went to rouse him saying, "Master! Master! We are going down!" Then he woke up and rebuked the wind and the rough water; and they subsided and it was calm again. He said to them, "Where is your faith?" They were awestruck and astonished and said to one another, "Who can this be, that gives orders even to winds and waves and they obey him?"[6]

Find a comfortable sitting position with your back balanced and erect. Close your eyes and be aware of your breath. Notice the sensations around your heart: weight, warmth, constriction, pleasure, numbness.

We believe that our mind is located in the head. But many Native American peoples laugh at this idea: according to their beliefs, the mind is located in the heart. In this meditation I invite you, also, to center your awareness in your heart.

Breathe deeply. And now, visualize your heart as a lake—a beautiful, round lake with deep, deep water: crystal clear, sparkling water. Far removed from the cities and dwellings of human beings, this lake lies alone, surrounded only by silence and the soft sounds of nature.

Take a look at your heart-lake. Look at the plants, the birds, the trees, the colors. Look up at the sky.

Now walk up to the very edge of the lake. There you find a small rowboat. It is loosely tied with a rope, and you know it is waiting for you. Notice its appearance, its color. This is your boat. So you untie the rope, throw it inside, and get in. With one oar you push off, and now you are gliding out over the lake.

You row out over the blue-green surface into the very center of the lake. This lake is your own heart. Its surface is an accurate reflection of your own inner state, which will vary according to your state of balance and tranquility. Sometimes, you may find the waves are quite rough, while at other times, just the slightest hint of a breeze will ruffle the calm surface. Notice the sky: is it cloudy and overcast, or clear and sunlit?

You are not simply at the mercy of wind and waves. Your breath is the instrument with which you can still your mind, soothe its turbulence, make it calm and peaceful. Watch this happening now as you breathe.

You can even clear the clouds from the sky, if you want. Floating in your boat, take as much time as you need to breathe, and, by the magic power of your breath, watch the lake becoming calm until its surface lies mirror-smooth and unbroken beneath a vast sky. Breathe, and watch the beauty of this lake. Receive fully the gift of peace and serenity.

Now as you look out over the lake, notice a swan. See its radiant white plumage, the elegant arch of its neck. It is in no hurry as it glides effortlessly over the calm water. See how it pauses to smooth some ruffled feathers, or to wet its beak.

Just watch the swan. Observe its peacefulness, grace, and ease. Floating free on the lake of your heart, you are the swan. You are consciousness, beauty, peace. You are silence.

Drink in the beauty of your own heart's scenery, the colors and sounds. And now slowly chant the following affirmations, either mentally or aloud:

I am peace.
I am beauty.
I am love.

I am peace.
I am beauty.
I am love.

Sit in meditation, resting in your heart-center for as long as you desire.

Give thanks to the lake for its pristine waters before returning to the world. Remember that you can return to this place anytime.

Breathe deeply. Feel your entire body. Gently stretch and move around. Try to maintain an awareness of your heart as a peaceful, open lake as you return to your activities.

Spirals of Ecstasy

RECOMMENDED MUSIC: Silence or meditation music

Sit in a comfortable position, with your back upright and unsupported. Lay both hands on your lap, palms up. Feel the earth below you, and inhale deeply a few times, drawing energy into the base of your spine.

Place your right hand on your lower abdomen, just above the pubic bone. Feel your weight, your earthiness. Let go into gravity. Visualize your pelvis as an open bowl resting on the earth, warm, relaxed, and gently caressed by your breath.

With your right arm, trace a large arc upward along the right side of your body. Moving in a wide half-circle, feel into the space right above your head and pause there for a few seconds. Envision light bursting forth from your head, crowning you with royalty from within. Reach into that glowing field of energy a couple of inches above your head and breathe the light through you.

And descending toward the left side of your body, continue your spiral until your right hand comes to rest on your navel center. This is your center, your source, and the center of the universe as well. Feel the fire that glows here, the contained power, and bless it with your touch.

Gently circling up to the right, around your face now, tenderly, as a mother's eyes encircle her child's face, move up around the right side of your face and gently lay your middle finger on your third eye, in the middle of the forehead. This is the eye of wisdom, the eye that sees not without but within. Bless the power of insight that resides within you.

Descend, reaching over to your left side, and spiraling gently in, lay your hand on your solar plexus, blessing your body with well-being, health, and contentment.

And following the spiral to the right and upward, gently touch your throat, blessing yourself with great creativity, with the power to communicate and express the wisdom that lies within you. Affirm your capacity to share your insight with others. And breathe.

And gliding slowly downward to the left, lay your hand gently on your heart. This is the throne of unconditional love and of healing compassion. Touch your heart lovingly, and breathe.

And having touched upon your heart's truth, reverse the spiral. Follow the spiral outward, up to the left, from your heart to your throat, to your solar plexus, third eye, navel, finally connecting sky and earth as you return from your crown chakra to the point above your pubic bone.

And, having returned, let your two hands rest together for some time. Feel how, with your movements, you have established your spine as a channel between earth and sky. Then, repeat the entire spiral, inward and outward, in the same way, but moving with your left arm. Then sit in silence for a few minutes.

Mindful Work

RECOMMENDED MUSIC: Silence

Choose a small activity that is easy and primarily physical: doing the dishes, cleaning, filing away some papers, making tea. First, choose quiet and solitary activities. Then try the same process while shopping in the supermarket, or talking on the telephone.

Make a commitment to perform this activity as spiritual practice, maintaining inner stillness and mindfulness throughout.

Let go of the compulsion to get your task finished and out of the way as quickly as possible. Instead, enter into your work as a sacred ritual. Move very slowly, and stay fully present with your movements, filling each one with beauty and grace. Follow your breath. Remember that in this moment nothing else in the world matters. If you are putting away a sweater, nothing matters but this movement of picking it up, folding it, and putting it in the closet. If you are washing a dish, nothing matters but the way you relate to its wet, gleaming surface.

If your mind wanders, bring it back to the breath. Stay present. Let yourself marvel at the beauty of your movements, their slow precision, the amazing coordination of hands and feet. These movements are your dance; enjoy them. If thoughts arise such as: "I don't like cleaning. I want to get it over with so I can do something enjoyable," then just notice this thought, neither judging yourself for having it, nor buying into it. Don't let your thoughts push you around. Realize that "I don't like cleaning" is just a theory, just an aspect of another self-image. It is an illusion, not the experience of the present moment.

Notice how attached your mind is to planning, commenting, how subtly it persuades you to run away. How difficult it is to stay present even for a single minute. And yet, how joyful it is to act from that space of radiant silence, how perfect, how peaceful. It takes practice, and it is worth practicing.

CHAPTER FOUR

Entering the Flow

The great sea
Has sent me adrift
It moves me
As the weed in a great river
Earth and the great weather
Move me
Have carried me away
And move my inward parts with joy.

SONG OF UVAVNUK,
ESKIMO WOMAN SHAMAN

The River of Life

THROUGHOUT TIME the great rivers of the world, from the Ganges to the Amazon, have been held sacred. And indeed the smallest stream we sit beside, listen to, and meditate upon will reveal itself as the sacred River of Life, and will teach us the principle of the *flow*. The power of the flow is the power to heal, rejuvenate, and purify, to dissolve hardened ego-structures, so that human beings can be made anew and reborn. Internally and externally, water is medicinal. Whether imbibed, bathed in, or contemplated, its healing power can be intensified by awareness and reverence for its essential purity.

Within nature, the flow ensures constant purification. To acknowledge the need for purification is not to imply that we are essentially impure, as Judeo-Christian doctrine suggests, but that the rightful place and function of all natural manifestations must be observed and honored. As one glance at our global environment reveals, we have produced far too many toxins—physical, mental, and emotional—and paid little or no attention to the need for purification. A most alarming measure of this disregard is the extent to which we have polluted the planet's waterways—yet another sign of our lack of reverence for the feminine. For is not water the feminine element of the womb in which the floating embryo dreams, and of the pregnant unconscious? Venus and Aphrodite, the goddesses of love and beauty, arise from the cosmic waters, as does their Indian counterpart, Lakshmi, goddess of abundance.

Sant Keshavadas, an Indian spiritual teacher, once told me a story about the Ganges river, which to Indians is the River of Life itself: sprung from the toe of God, the Ganges danced down over the matted locks of Shiva, who broke the great fall of the river's waters with his head, so that in her power the river would not injure the earth. At one time, heavy rain formed a small pond right next to the Ganges. It had a little water, and soon became proud and began preaching to the river Ganges: "O river, don't waste all that water by pouring it into the ocean, which already has more than enough. Hold it back! Preserve your water!" At this, the Ganges laughed and said to the pond: "I am given in abundance, therefore I give. If I stopped flowing, God would withhold his flow from me. Therefore learn from me that life must flow. Thoughts must flow, energy must flow, love must flow, money must flow." But the pond refused to listen. Like a mantra, it kept repeating: "Hold on, preserve!" After a few days, some women came and washed their dirty laundry in the pond. Then some buffalo came and wallowed in the pond, and finally the scorching Indian sun dried up all the water until the pond, having no springs of its own, disappeared entirely. But the Ganges still dances down into the ocean. And as it flows, it sings: *Aum Tatsat Aum. Aum Tatsat Aum.* God alone is Truth. God alone is Truth. Glory be to God.

The Flow of Life-force within the Human Being

Energy must flow, the Ganges tells us. This is in short the most basic law of both movement meditation and of all healing. Flow is health and wholeness, and its absence causes stagnation and *dis-ease*. In this chapter, we will discuss some aspects of relating to pain as a form of blockage, as well as ways of maintaining and balancing the flow of life-force through breath, voice, and movement.

Our life-force, reverentially called *prana* by the Indians and *chi* by the Chinese, is immeasurably subtle yet undeniably present. It streams through our body like rivers flow through a fertile country; such internal rivers are called *nadis* in the Yogic system; Chinese medicine speaks of meridian lines. Most Eastern healing systems claim that health depends on the balance and harmony of the body's internal flows, and that, through the mindful practice of the body's natural wave movements combined with the gentle rhythm of breath, it is possible to influence and rebalance them.

Western medicine, despite its obvious successes, is still limited by its discarding of all data that cannot be confirmed by objective measurement. As a result, it does not consider the internal flows known to Eastern medicine. Though the instruments of modern technology are sophisticated in detecting physical signs of illness, they are extremely crude compared to the subtlety of the human body and its energy systems. Through movement meditation, however, you can rediscover some of these internal flows for yourself, provided you move slowly and mindfully, following your breath and allowing your body to lead the way. All external movement energizes the internal flows of energy, but only when you are centered in stillness and in a heightened state of bodily awareness can you actually feel them. Movement meditation helps us to refine our awareness, so that we can feel and connect with the tiny ripples and subtle streams of energy within us.

Pain as a Call for Change

Pain is not God's way of punishing us; rather, it is the body's way of requesting change. Something is stuck, stagnant, and needs to return to the flow. If you are trying to heal yourself of a chronic condition or a serious disease, I would strongly advise that in addition to medical treatment you seek out a person trained to help you access the healing powers of your own body. Many techniques serve this aim, and an increasing number of therapists and healing professionals are working in the area of self-healing. A person who understands the emotional aspects of bodywork should be able to support you in fully contacting and integrating the unfinished issues that support your illness. It is not enough to simply understand these issues intellectually. In the willingness to physically and emotionally explore the experience of pain, a compassionate embracing of yourself occurs, which is essential to healing. You emerge with a better understanding of yourself and a new level of awareness in the very cells of your body.

The body often acts out learned behavior totally inappropriate to the present moment. Perhaps, fifty years ago, your father beat you, and your brain gave your shoulders the command to curl protectively around the heart. At the time, that was a sensible thing to do. But half a century later, your shoulders are still tight, and probably painful. Though every cell of your body has been replaced many times since then, the old information has been handed down from one generation of muscle tissue to the next. Healing requires that old mental defenses, as well as harmful physical conditioning, be dissolved back into the flow. The very act of defending yourself against pain may be one of the main causes of your suffering.

If you are in physical pain, try to enter a state of deep relaxation and communicate directly with your body. Ask what caused it to get sick, and what changes it is requesting. Physical pain does not necessarily stem from physical causes, but may be the result of previously ignored emotional or spiritual needs. Healing may involve something as simple as rest or as complex as a radical change of lifestyle and environment. Unfortunately, even in the face of life-threatening disease, when resistance to change may prove fatal, not everyone is willing to stop and listen to the body's messages.

In America, the typical response to pain is to grab a painkiller. But when you honor pain as a teacher, you will no longer be so eager to kill it, for when the we deaden the pain, we also deaden the potential insight it has to offer. Arnold Mindell, a brilliant therapist and bodyworker, insists on the necessity of respecting the body's pain as a valid form of self-expression, and criticizes the prevailing medical establishment for its approach toward pain as something to be killed off as efficiently and promptly as possible:

> But the most immediate result of the ailing healing attitude is that it suffocates potential consciousness and development. Many body messages expound violent existential warnings about the necessity for instantaneous change. If these messages are consistently blurred with pain killers, relaxants and surgery, psychological death results. Then human beings are turned into robots directed by the frail so-called scientific consciousness of others.[1]

Emotional Flow

The word *emotion* comes from Latin *emovere,* to move out. Emotions are energy, and energy is, by its very nature, always flowing, shifting, and moving. Emotion is linked to *expression,* a term that literally means that which pushes out. Unless we hold them back, emotions will naturally find the appropriate form of expression through movement. Movement implies change: by allowing an emotion to move, we open the way for it to transform into something new. Repression, on the other hand, freezes it into immobility. The problem with repressed emotions is not the nature of the emotions themselves, for there is no such thing as a "bad" emotion. The problem is that frozen emotions cannot flow, and therefore they stagnate and fester instead of transforming.

Emotional expression in itself, however, does not guarantee personal growth. A river has not run its full course until it reaches the ocean, and the flow of emotion is incomplete until all the darkness of fear, anger, guilt, and pain has been transformed into light. People tend to become addicted to the emotions they are familiar with, and thus a person may become attached to her anger, or pain, or whatever her specialty happens to be. Therapy that encourages emotional expression without fostering spiritual awareness runs the risk of locking clients into dramatic but ultimately unproductive patterns of emotional catharsis. Such emotional addiction is a distorted expression of the spirit's unmet need for love, and it is only through the experience of unconditional love that the individual is able to allow the transformation and release of familiar but painful emotional patterns.

Blocked emotional pain often causes the heart area to feel numb, dead, stiff, or sore, and may even create physiological heart problems. Though we speak of a "closed" heart, it is never closed, only enclosed by unprocessed emotion. Through breath, voice, and movement, especially through rocking and singing, you can touch and massage your heart from within. Don't hold back your tears; rather, think of them as the pain a frostbitten limb feels when it begins to thaw near the warmth of a fire. Keep moving through your heart pain, and it will transform into love.

Suffering as Initiation and Purification

As a teenager wandering through European churches and museums, Christianity seemed a very morbid religion, obsessed with the gruesome suffering of crucifixion and with countless images of martyrdom. But I later realized that suffering and holiness are universally associated. Every spiritual mythology includes stories of holy men and women who undergo tremendous anguish for which there is no obvious necessity.

Suffering becomes unbearable only when it is perceived as meaningless. How then do we find meaning within our suffering? First we must realize that meaning derives from spiritual, not intellectual, sources and is founded not on logical reasoning but on an intuitive act of faith. A sense of meaning is won through struggling with suffering and the cosmic forces responsible for it, moving through the pain, the grief, the anger, the confusion. Like Job, we should not meekly capitulate, but always insist on God's accountability and our right to know God. Though Job is never given any rational explanation of his trials, he finally makes peace with life when, through his struggle, he arrives at a stage where he can fully and wholeheartedly say "yes" to all that is and has been.

Christians have traditionally been taught that they are sinners, that their sins caused Christ's anguish, and that suffering is their just dessert. Such doctrine is bound to foster feelings of guilt and unworthiness. Shamanic traditions hold a different point of view; they consider suffering a necessary stage of transition, comparable to labor during childbirth. Shamanic initiations into a higher level of creative power may also involve great suffering, but this suffering carries no implication of guilt or sin. Through pain, the shaman bursts through the shell of ego and is born into cosmic consciousness—and is, in this way, initiated into the spiritual sources of physical life so that he or she may become a healer.

The experience of being physically dismembered is a traditional prerequisite to shamanic re-membering, and shamans often describe the experience of their own dismemberment in gruesome detail. Some are ripped apart and devoured by wild beasts who later become their power animals. Some are killed, cut apart, and sometimes even cooked by spirits. Some are shot, starved, frozen, or drowned. But as consciousness expands and the ultimate unity of existence is realized, these wounds of dismemberment heal.

Here, suffering forcibly breaks apart the rigid structure of the individual's ego. One is touched by the hand of a greater power, not with a caress but with a blow, and yet, such suffering is a mark of divine grace, a calling to service. In the Acts of John, declared heretical by the Catholic church in

447 C.E., Jesus' own suffering is described in terms similar to those used in accounts of shamanic initiation; Christ's anguish is real on one plane, yet unreal on the higher plane to which he has ascended:

> So then I have suffered none of those things which they will say of me;
> even that suffering which I showed to you and to the rest in my dance,
> I will that it be called a mystery.[2]

Traditional psychotherapy often betrays the patient by failing to acknowledge that his or her suffering may have spiritual—as well as emotional and mental—causes, or by attempting to interpret the pain of spiritual hunger as an emotional problem. Obviously, we are not all destined to become shamans or healers; not all pain is symptomatic of spiritual awakening. Nonetheless, every major experience of suffering must be approached as a spiritual initiation. The need for spiritual growth is genuine and at times may surface with great urgency. At such times, the individual who does not heed her soul's call may well fall ill. The shamanic view of suffering invites us to relate to our body as a messenger of personal evolution and inner growth, and to approach suffering not as punishment for our sins, but rather as doorways into expanded states of consciousness.

The Flow of Breath

In using movement to dissolve blockages and purify the internal rivers of our life-force, we must understand that the subtler the movement, the greater its healing power. Breath is therefore an extremely powerful healing tool, as well as the most important sign of the flow of life-force in our bodies. Spirit, from the Latin *spirare* (to breathe), is the breath of God, breath the flow of spirit. The wave movement of breath, like the serpent, is associated with the most primitive manifestations of life, as well as with the highest states of enlightenment. Both voluntary and involuntary breathing allow us to access otherwise inaccessible regions of the psyche. Thich Nhat Hanh says:

Our breath is the bridge from our body to our mind, the element which reconciles our body and mind and which makes possible one-ness of body and mind. Breath is aligned to both body and mind and it alone is the tool which can bring them both together, illuminating both and bringing both peace and calm.[3]

Cultivating awareness of breath can tremendously increase the healing impact of meditative movement. Simply being conscious of your breath is far more important that any specific technique. If you begin to observe your breathing, you will be amazed at how often you stop, or breathe so shallowly that your body barely gets the minimum amount of oxygen it needs. As long as your breath flows freely, you are probably not blocking the flow elsewhere. If you find yourself holding your breath, ask yourself what else is being held back—a tense muscle? Thoughts, words, tears, laughter? Begin by simply committing yourself to noticing your breathing at least three times a day. By establishing this habit, you begin to develop greater awareness of your breath throughout the day.

The Hindus have a monkey god whose name is Hanuman. Hanuman

Hanuman, the monkey god, symbol of cosmic life-force and breath. Cambodia, circa 930 C.E.

represents prana—the cosmic life-force, and the vital energy that monkeys possess so abundantly. The monkey god symbolically personifies the power of breath, and is also known as the "son of the wind." The Hanuman Chalisa, a hymn sung in praise of the monkey god, describes how he guards the door to enlightenment, and claims that without his blessing no one can experience God-consciousness. Within the body, his energy is stored in the navel center and circulated through the breath to all parts of the body. Like Hanuman, our breath is the doorkeeper of enlightenment:

> Kabir says: Student, tell me, what is God?
> He is the breath inside the breath.[4]

One of the great Hindu epics, the *Ramayana,* tells the story of how God and Goddess incarnated on earth and lived as husband and wife. One day, however, a great demon abducts the Goddess. Both she and her divine husband despair until the monkey god Hanuman finds her and, acting as a messenger between the divine couple, helps reunite them.

This myth is the story of our own spiritual path. Within our body, the serpentine goddess lies coiled in the root chakra at the base of our spine;[5] her Sanskrit name is *Kundalini,* the Coiled One. The potential for enlightened consciousness in the crown of the head is personified as Rama, the male aspect of the divine. The goal of spiritual evolution is the sacred marriage between Goddess and God, the wedding of our physical life-force and our spirit. This union within ourselves is obstructed by the demon of our ignorance who abducts and imprisons our energy, and tries to sabotage the process of our awakening. But we have an ally in our breath. When we begin to meditate, our breath anchors us in the truth of the present moment. As Hanuman became the messenger between God and Goddess in the *Ramayana,* so our breath gently guides the great river of energy through the spinal column, leading the way to the mystic marriage.

The Flow of Voice

Though we rarely think of our voice as a form of movement, sounding and chanting are actually very important elements of movement meditation, which provide the body with a subtle but very powerful internal massage.

Your voice is the vehicle by which your individual energy transmits itself to the world. Crying, screaming, singing, and shouting all belong to the flow of energy. But many adults have lost their voice. The voice they speak with is merely a censored, stymied remnant of their true voice, which they lost as children by assimilating the spoken or unspoken rules of their family: don't cry, don't make any sound if you do cry, don't show your fear, don't express your anger. Many people never find the voice of their pain, or the voice of their rage. Many women, afraid to own the full range of their adult emotionality and power, hide behind the tiny voice of a little girl.

The human voice is a transmitter not only of information, but of spiritual vibration. Sometimes the quality of a person's voice affects us more than the actual words they say. Two people may tell you the same thing, but you will believe one and not the other, because her voice rings of truth. When the vibration of one's personal body-mind is fully aligned with the cosmic truth, one's voice becomes what the Hindu calls *mantric,* resonant with sacred power. Certain spiritual teachers initiate their students through the transmission of spiritual vibration carried by the vehicle of their voice. You may actually find the quality of your voice changing as a result of regular chanting practice.

Any form of singing is healing, but chanting is especially beneficial because it generally involves concentration on a positive image or thought, so that the mind is being saturated with positive vibrations and swept clean of all else. Chanting aligns body, mind, and spirit and gently removes all kinds of subtle impurities. In mystical experience, there is no difference between the deity and the deity's name; to sing or chant the holy name is to evoke the holy presence. According to creation myths of many cultures, the world began with vibration (or, as in Genesis, with "the word of God") and consists of vibration. Sound is vibration, and vibration is the basic stuff of which we are made.

Like all forms of rhythmic vibration, the voice is a natural consciousness-altering tool. Consider for instance the shaman's use of power songs. Among certain tribes, everyone possesses a death song, a song sung throughout life like a personal prayer or mantra. By the time a person dies, this song has taken such deep roots in their consciousness that it can be counted on as a source of comfort, encouragement, and support as they pass through the gates of death.

You may discover that you, too, have power songs. They may come to you unexpectedly, or you can search for them and invite them through an intense period of spiritual commitment. But, even if you keep singing for days, you cannot force a power song to come to you. Whether you think you "can sing" or not does not matter at all. Your power song is given to you by sources beyond the comprehension of your mind. Often, power songs are extremely simple, with only a few words or no words at all. A power song is a precious gift; it stays with you forever. Whenever you sing it, it will reconnect you with your inner resources of strength and faith.

Dancing with the Flow

Flow and change are synonymous. The air we breathe, the food we eat, the cells of our body come and go. The entire universe meanders through our thoughts, and yet we possess nothing permanently. With nothing to lose, you are free, and change is easy to accept. The fact that we are attached to so many things and feel we have so much to lose—possessions, comforts, lovers, health, jobs—makes us, like the small pond next to the Ganges, hold on tight, clinching our fists and bracing ourselves against possible calamity.

Right now, the world is transforming at an accelerated speed, so it is essential that we master the art of gracefully surrendering to change. Globally, this is a period of transition and change; everyone is affected in one way or another, and no environment, however secluded, is exempt. Attempting to control these changes is like trying to maneuver against whitewater rapids, or like trying to catch a snake as it slithers full speed through the underbrush. The only solution is to go along with the flow of the river, to *become* the snake.

The body, also, has only two ways of reacting to change. It can contract, rigidify, and tighten, or it can move, release higher levels of energy, and thereby relax. Major changes can either deplete us or they can energize us. As you grapple with a particularly intense experience, you may find yourself tightening in an instinctive attempt to take control of the situation. People can literally become petrified by fear. The problem is not the tensing itself, but the fact that the tension is never fully released, so that remnants of the original fear still remain present in the body to sap one's energy. Instead of resisting and contracting in the face of change, as we so often do, we need to open up and become more fluid and loose.

If a snake merely contracted and never expanded, it could never move forward. A snake's movement depends on the interplay of opposites: tension and release, contraction and expansion. Similarly, we must allow the tension we accumulate in our bodies to be released, which is best achieved by working with trembling and shaking movements. Change may cause anxiety and tension; therefore, the more your life is in a process of transition and transformation, the more important it is that you consciously befriend the serpent by opening your body to the flow of change through movement and dance. When the river runs fast and wild, you must learn to surrender: fight the current, and you go under.

Grace

It is no coincidence that we use the word *grace* both to describe physical beauty of movement and for a state of spiritual blessedness. When life-energy flows in its fullness though any living being, it manifests internally as pleasure and externally as grace. Grace and pleasure are natural attributes of the sacred. Every time you ignore what gives your body pleasure, you lose some of the grace that every child and every wild animal possesses in such abundance.

Grace is a wonderful word, one of the few in the English language that stands at the intersection of the physical and the spiritual, reminding us that our task as human beings is not simply to identify ourselves as spiritual beings, but to embody spirit. Grace is the fruit of such embodiment.

The Body of Bliss

All living creatures instinctively strive to maintain their health. Health manifests internally as a sense of well-being and externally as grace. Beyond that, human beings have the potential to break out of the boundaries of their personal self into oneness with the cosmos, as Uvavnuk did. Her shamanic song ecstatically bursts forth from the confinement of the ego-self into the great River of Life. No longer standing high and dry on the riverbank, she has immersed herself unconditionally, allowing herself to be dissolved and carried away by the great River.

Sacred dance can transport you into the ecstatic consciousness of knowing your oneness with All That Is. Your body may expand to include animals and people, rivers, forests, mountains, and galaxies. But loving our body can become simply yet another form of egotistical indulgence unless we understand clearly that the appropriate object of our love is not an individual body in isolation, but that our own body is sacred only as a part of the cosmic body, the unlimited whole. The Buddhists call this ecstatic recognition of the oneness of existence *Sambhogakaya,* the body of bliss. *Sam* means all together; *bhoga* means enjoyment, bliss; and *kaya* means body. Sambhogakaya therefore literally means the joy of knowing that everything belongs to a single body; the joy of knowing oneness, not as an intellectual concept, but a physical experience.

Every spiritual tradition has its own terminology for describing the same experience. The theologian Matthew Fox defines the Cosmic Christ as "the pattern that connects."[6] Some teachers like Jean Houston speak of the universe as a giant hologram,[7] and Buddhist Thich Nhat Hanh calls this mutual connectedness "interbeing."[8]

Whatever name we give it, this recognition of the oneness of existence is a concept both spiritual, ecological, and political. It is not just a philosophical idea, but a powerful and essential foundation for creating peace on earth. From the realization of the interconnectedness of our bodies with all other bodies' compassion, commitment to the well-being of others and an understanding of the futility of warfare are born. Though we may cling to the illusion of our individual independence, we are in fact interdependent in every detail of our life. Whatever happens in one area of the universe affects all other parts. For instance, when the nuclear reactor at Chernobyl erupted, radiation did not halt at national borders. Within just a few hours, it had reached the Canadian Arctic. Whether we are aware of it or not, each one of us is merely a wave that has no separate existence apart from the river. We can protect ourselves only be protecting the entire river.

Awareness of continuity within nature leads to a sense of our responsibility for how we live in the world. An invisible thread connects each moment to the next, creating what we call causality, or *karma,* the law of cause and effect. Our movements never arise randomly or in isolation. We move, and although we may not always possess the knowledge to discriminate accurately, what we have set into motion may be beneficial or detrimental to others; it may cause suffering or bring healing. When you understand this dynamic, you understand that your movements really matter. By moving peacefully and consciously you become a source of peace to the world.

CHAPTER FOUR: MEDITATIONS

Entering the Flow

RECOMMENDED MUSIC: Meditation music or very gentle rhythmic music

This meditation can also be practiced in a sitting position and is suitable for people using wheelchairs.

Stand, close your eyes, and breathe. Find the right place for your feet, a place from where they can reach into the earth like a plant putting down roots.

Now, I invite you to imagine that you are completely immersed in a gently flowing river. The water is a pleasant temperature, and you can easily breathe in it. This is no ordinary water. It is a river of crystal clear, healing light.

Even your breath is of this sparkling, healing light. Breathe it in and let it fill your lungs. Breathing out, feel it filling your entire body.

Standing in a river of light, water moving all around you in gentle currents, become like a plant yourself, your entire body flexible and yielding.

As you breathe, let the water flow over your skin and caress you. Feel the currents nudging you, maybe gently turning your head to the side, or making your hips rotate ever so slightly with the flow.

Begin to let yourself be moved by the river without and the currents within. As if in a dream, let yourself enter the enchantment of the underwater world.

Images of fish or other water creatures may float through your vision. Become one among them, drifting along. Or a water plant, swaying in the current. Or a pebble, rolling around gently on the ocean floor.

Close your eyes as you move. There is water all around you, and water within you. There is not that much difference between your body and the water around you. You, too, are fluid and soft.

Keep moving. Breathe deeply and allow breath to swirl through the inside spaces of your body. Let out some deep sighs. Sense the resistance of the water around you. It won't allow you to move very fast. Just relax and surrender your body to the flow. Let the water caress your body.

Don't work at this. You have worked hard enough. Let the water move you. Let your body melt, dissolve, disintegrate into the streaming.

The less you interfere with your dance, the better. Just enjoy the currents as they come and pass through you. Feel the luxury of melting into the water. Let your whole being melt. Become soft and yielding, no resistance anywhere.

Your movements are slow, dreamlike. In this dimension, time has no meaning. Only the present is meaningful, the melting of your body into the currents, and your slow dance with the river.

The more completely you surrender, the more you will find that the difference between what is inside of you and what is outside dissolves. The waters flow around you and through you, merging with your blood, your heartbeat. Become a piece of seaweed, swaying with the current.

Every time you release a particle of tension, a tightness in your body lets go and a new kernel of sweetness unfolds within. There is more space inside, and so movement is easier. Simply let the currents move you—no effort. Let your body move softly, like a wave, a water plant, a fish. Let yourself be turned and twisted, rolled around.

The waters without merge with the waters within. Trust their power to wash you clean, to baptize you, to make you new. Breathe through you the healing currents. Let these waters determine your movement. Become totally receptive to the healing light.

Move in this way for about fifteen minutes. Then, sit down in a comfortable position, keeping your back upright. The flow of breath continues. Notice how your body feels now. Let the movement continue, but in a very subtle, inward way, almost invisibly.

Still, everything around you undulates and sways. You are surrounded and held by loving, healing energy. Breathe and let go. Know that you are at home in this universe.

Pain Meditation

RECOMMENDED MUSIC: Silence or meditation music

Find a comfortable position in which you can relax fully.

> Notice your pain. Notice the sensations that surround it, sensations of throbbing or burning, cold or heat.
>
> The more it hurts, the more you probably clinch in defense. The muscles around the pain form a ring of defense, tightening, trying to isolate the pain, to put it in quarantine.
>
> And your mind, too, has perhaps clinched and become hard and angry. "Why me?" you may ask. And, "No! Go away! I don't want you. Stop it! Let me be!"
>
> But the pain remains, and you have declared war on it. You have set the boundaries, fortified them with lines of tension, and established the enemy. You are vigilant, wary.
>
> But ultimately, this hardening does not serve you. In fact, it intensifies the pain and prevents healing. The element of healing is water: soft, fluid, water that flows around the hardness, gently but surely dissolving it.
>
> So, just for the next few minutes, try to let down your defenses against the pain. Try to stop relating to it as an enemy. Instead, just let yourself feel it, be with it. If you are willing to do this, there is a possibility of communicating with the pain, perhaps even softening it.
>
> Let go of labeling the sensations in your body. Be willing to simply perceive them, without fighting back.
>
> Let your breathing be cool and fluid and gentle. Follow the breath as it flows into the hurting areas. Like an infinitely loving touch, allow it to flow around the edges of your pain. Like water flowing over hard, crusted mud, let your breath begin to soften the tightness.
>
> When you inhale, direct your breath flow into the areas of pain. When you exhale, let go. Let go deeper. Stop struggling. Stop fighting the pain.

Be aware of the parts of your body that are not in pain, and fill them with breath. Notice where there is pleasure in your body and where there is pain, and feel how both can co-exist.

Breathe, and let your heart soften, let your belly soften. Imagine that the pain is being held within a space of warm, infinitely loving energy. All around, the pain is surrounded by this spacious, loving field.

Notice whether there is any fear connected with the pain: fear of it continuing forever, fear of death, of poverty, of isolation, of the unknown future.

Sometimes we get so accustomed to living with fear that we think it quite natural. But fear is an extremely toxic substance. It makes you contract, denying you the peace of mind available in every moment.

Fear is deceptive, disguising itself in seemingly rational logic. It says to you, "You have cause for fear. You have to watch out! Choose me, and I will protect you!"

Your clear assessment of the truth is indeed helpful and allows you to make the right choices for yourself. But your fear has never helped you. Fear inhibits the healing process, though it claims to protect you. Fear is part of the disease.

Open your heart to sadness, if sadness is present. Allow the healing waters to soften your heart and wash through your eyes. Let the sadness flow through you. Honor the grief for what has been lost. No tightening in the chest against the sobbing. If it arises, just let it wash through. Let the sadness come and go, neither resisting it or getting attached.

And every time you notice your body tightening in defense around the pain, gently breathe through. Encourage your body to let go, dissolving, dissolving.

Your body is not as solid as it seems. Every molecule is floating within vast, empty space. Send your breath into these empty spaces; with your breath, send love for yourself, compassion for yourself. Let every molecule be held and supported by love on all sides.

By tightening, you reject your body when it most needs your love. Understand that the tightening does not help. On the contrary, it only supports the pain by giving it an illusion of solidity. In fact, there is nothing solid about your pain. This pain is not an object, not a thing. By considering it a solid entity, you empower it.

More and more, breathe into the very center of your pain. Let your breath carry you inwards, gently, without any force, until you arrive in the very heart of pain. Breathe compassion for yourself through the pain.

Like a fish at home in the depths of the ocean, let yourself float free in your body. As you breathe, flow with the healing currents around and through the pain. Keep melting and dissolving. No hardening, no contracting, no need to defend. Let everything in you dissolve into acceptance of what is. Just being with yourself, compassionately, lovingly. Breathe.

Let all the tensions float away in the water like driftwood. Watch them swirling into the distance and let your mind relax its control.

Now begin to talk to your body. If possible, speak out loud. If this is not appropriate, speak mentally. Say something of this nature to your body:

> Body, I am here. I am with you. I am listening to you. Please communicate with me. Let me know whether there is anything you want of me. I cannot promise that I will do whatever you ask of me, but I am willing to hear your voice and respect your wishes.

Now breathe, and silence your mind as much as possible. For now, set aside the doubting, skeptical voice and be receptive and open-minded like a child. Just listening into your body.

Your body may respond to you in words, or it may respond in images, colors. The response may be minimal and confusing, or it may be crystal clear, startling.

Be willing to hear whatever your body says. You do not need to obey it. But if you are able to hear your body's voice, you will be able to make conscious choices around it. To hear your body's voice is to take responsibility for your own healing, to empower yourself as the healer.

Speak with your body as long as you want. Ask it the questions you need to ask. Then just breathe through. For a few more minutes, just breathe and stay with the sense of opening and softening, of compassionately being present in the vast and mysterious territory of your own body.

Sacred Space

RECOMMENDED MUSIC: Silence or meditation music

Sit comfortably, with your back upright, or lie down. Observe your breath without interfering.

Notice as you breathe in, what was outside of you becomes inside. And as you breathe out, what was inside of you flows out.

Your breathing is a dialogue between you and the outside world. With every breath, this communication is continuing. Normally, you think of this breathing as "your" breath. Now, explore something new.

Imagine for a moment that this breath is not yours. Imagine that it is a force of its own that swings back and forth between you and the universe. It flows into your body as you inhale and flows into the world as you exhale.

So, for now, see if you can release the notion that this breathing process is something you own. Just observe it as a gentle swinging between your body and the universe.

Breath flows from you, and is received by the universe. Breath flows from the universe, and is received by you. When you breathe out, the universe breathes in. When you breathe in, the universe breathes out.

Gently, patiently, allow yourself to open to this communication. Let it deepen, until the breath moves between your heart and the heart of the universe.

Your heart and the heart of the universe breathing one another.

Breath is life. Breath is spirit. When the breath leaves the body, the spirit leaves. When breath enters, life enters.

What is touched by breath is touched by spirit; it becomes sacred. Therefore as the breath flows into your body, affirm to yourself: this is sacred space. Touched by breath, my body is receiving the blessing of spirit.

And, as the breath flows outward into the heart of the universe, say to yourself: this, too, is sacred space, blessed by the movement of breath, blessed by the flow of divine spirit.

Inhaling, say: sacred space within.
Exhaling, say: sacred space without.

Continue for at least fifteen minutes.

Singing the Soul

RECOMMENDED MUSIC: Your own voice

This meditation should be done in an environment in which you feel free to make as much noise as you want. It can be adapted to other situations, but this entails a loss in terms of your ability to drop all self-consciousness and lose yourself entirely in the process.

Also, time should be no consideration. It may take you only a few minutes to claim your voice, but sometimes it takes several hours. Enter into this process with an attitude of patience and receptivity toward yourself.

Don't fool yourself into thinking you are done when you are actually just standing at an edge, at a cliff. It is easy to confuse these edges with tiredness, or boredom, to believe nothing is happening. For this reason it really helps to have a group of people when doing this meditation, people who have the patience to stay attentive to your process, who will cheer you on when you get stuck and get excited with you when you break through.

Begin in any comfortable position you choose.

Your intention in this meditation is to set your soul free to express itself. The soul does not speak in the same language as the rational mind. Its language is song, poetry, dance—the language of the heart.

The less your mind interferes, the more freedom your soul will have to find its own voice. Try to release all expectations of singing well, of being creative, of having exciting experiences.

Move while you sing. Never let your body become rigid. Keep shifting, swaying, dancing. Stay open to the currents. Breathe. Notice your exhalations. Gradually let them become more audible, like a sigh.

Allow the sigh to become a sound—for now, just an "aaaaahhh . . ."; no more. No particular pitch, no song. Let go of trying to control your voice. No pushing, no trying to keep the sound even, or use up all the breath. Just the sound of "aaaaahhh. . . ."

On every single exhalation *without exception,* let your voice stream out. Don't stop or pause. Just keep going, noticing what happens, but not interfering.

Observe: does your voice sound full and resonant, or compressed and tight? Do you feel the vibration throughout your body, in your belly, or only in your upper chest and throat? Follow the sound, let it explore different places inside you. Explore the unfamiliar and the unknown—whatever happens, don't stop!

Your body is an instrument, like a cello or a flute. Your voice vibrates every part of it. In a naturally relaxed body, you can feel the whole chest and abdomen vibrating. Your whole body becomes a resonating chamber, vibration touching and harmonizing every part.

But we cut ourselves off from certain places by tightening the muscles in these parts. So when we sing, the tight places can't vibrate and resonate with the sound. When you notice resistance, don't push your breath through it forcibly. Rather, question it gently, exploring the edges.

Your voice has the power to touch upon all these areas. It has the power to gently massage them, vibrate the numb areas back to life, penetrate the thick defenses.

So let your voice begin to explore the inside of your body. If you feel the resonance in your throat, see if you could let it fill your chest, too. If your voice fills your chest, see if you can allow it to fill your entire abdomen.

Let your body sway and swing with your song. Get up and dance, or crawl on the floor and let those old noises out: child noises, animal noises, snarling, howling, keening noises.

Tell your mind to rest, to step aside, to quit criticizing and censoring. Give over your voice to your soul. Set it free to sing its longing, its pain, its love. Use all the sounds that are stored away inside of you, waiting for an opportunity to come out. Words are not necessary. But if words well up that want to be sung, let them sing themselves.

Perhaps your song is right there, waiting to be sung. Perhaps you feel barren, songless. Persevere. Often, what seems like barrenness is just the gatekeeper to the realm of your song. Sometimes, you must be willing to linger in the shadows for a long time, waiting. Just opening to the voice, giving it space, freedom, permission. Not pushing, not demanding anything, but also not withdrawing. Keep singing. Just as your breath always flows, so continue to let your voice flow with it.

And feel the presence of the universal spirit, the holy spirit, the soul of the universe. To this Presence dedicate your song. Let your soul sing itself completely, holding nothing back, neither your anger, your sense of betrayal, your confusion, your loneliness, nor your joy, your silliness, your tenderness. Sing everything that is. Sing your lament as well as your praise. Sing the truth.

Keep singing until you really know you are done. Then, your song will melt down into silence, silence that is not the opposite of song, but was part of your song all along.

In this silence, listen to the Presence. Listen, in the silence, to the ringing hum of the world singing itself into being.

CHAPTER FIVE

Gut Wisdom

Tanden [the navel center] is the shrine of the Divine. If its stronghold is finely built so that the Divine in us can grow then a real human being is achieved. If one divides people into ranks the lowest is he who values his head. Those who endeavor only to amass as much knowledge as possible grow heads that become bigger and so they topple over easily, like a pyramid standing upside down. They excel in imitating others but neither originality nor inventiveness nor any great work is theirs.

Next come those of middle rank. For them the chest is most important. People with self-control, given to abstinence and asceticism belong to this type. These are the men with outward courage but without real strength. Many of the so-called great men are in this category. Yet all this is not enough.

But those who regard the belly as the most important part and so have built the stronghold where the Divine can grow—these are the people of the highest rank. They have developed their minds as well as their bodies in the right way. Strength flows out from them and produces a spiritual condition of ease and equanimity. They do what seems good to them without violating any law. Those in the first category think that Science can rule Nature. Those in the second have apparent courage and discipline and they know how to fight. Those in the third know what reality is.

MASTER OKADA TORAJIRO

The Hara

W HEN CHILDREN BEGIN to draw, they portray the human figure as a head resting on a circle. Only later will they add arms and legs. The body is first experienced as a round form, a mandala; its center lies in the belly, a few inches below the navel. The Japanese call this center point the Hara, and they consider it the core of the human being, the seed around which a child's sense of self will unfold. Recently while I was shopping in a local market, a beaming two-year-old child approached me. "I am me!" he declared, patting his belly with pride. He had discovered his center, his Hara.

The Hara is the easiest, most effortless and natural point from which to move. The grace of an African dancer, and the dignity of many tribal people stems from their centeredness in Hara. Every living creature knows its center instinctively; even when lost this knowledge can be consciously rediscovered. Centering in the belly grants us a sense of power, balance, and clarity. Gravity connects our navel to the earth's center; instead of fighting this pull, we respond to it in the most direct, efficient way. In many traditional Eastern forms of movement meditation and martial arts, the beginner's first step is to learn to rest in the navel center. An ungrounded person wastes a great deal of energy fighting gravity and easily loses balance, but a well-grounded person stands solidly on the earth and cannot be easily toppled. Settling our consciousness in the navel center is a basic spiritual, mental, physical discipline; developing an unshakable foundation may require years of practice.

The pelvis, in relation to the body, may be likened to the foundation of a tall house; although the roof may offer a more dramatic view, the base is no less essential to the building's integrity. Gut wisdom, emanating from the pelvic region, provides the basis for great practical insight, allowing us to perceive reality clearly. While the human body reflects our personal truth, the ground upon which we stand represents a planetary truth, a larger reality to which we must respond. To be *grounded* refers to our connection with the earth itself, but also with the ground of reality. Our stance expresses how firmly our personal truth is rooted in universal truth: centered in the pelvis, respecting our gut wisdom, we can approach reality in a direct, lucid manner; we can breathe deeply and rest peacefully in our center.

The Process of Repression

The pelvis acts as an internal fireplace, sometimes suffused with an aura of well-being as food becomes fuel, sometimes kindling the flames of sexual passion, sometimes flaring up in aggression driving us to fight tooth and nail for survival. Not surprisingly, animals shield the vital organs of the belly and pelvic area by walking on all four legs. The fact that human beings expose the body's most vulnerable part to the world is a significant indicator of the unique spiritual challenge we face—the challenge of living in constant awareness of life's fragility and of developing compassion for ourselves and others.

Gut feelings are designed to help us survive individually and as a species. They alert us to the presence of danger and trigger important self-protective reactions. Ironically, the most powerful self-preserving instincts we possess—anger and sexuality—are the least socially acceptable, and quite early in life we learn to view these feelings as dangerous troublemakers. Confronted with a large, angry adult, children quickly learn to build a cage within their belly into which they stuff their own fear and rage. Furthermore, parents hand on their own sexual shame to their children, and shame too is held as tension within the pelvic area. A sexually abused child may associate sexual feelings with such an unbearable sense of betrayal and rage that such feelings are blocked off entirely, easily done by tightening the pelvic area.

Repression occurs whenever the values of any outside authority are established as internal command-givers. These may be the values of parents and teachers, but also of society as a whole. Our society in particular rewards those who are successful, self-reliant, and militantly independent.

Learning to ask for what we need, whether it be acknowledgement, love, sex, or money, is for many of us an encounter with old experiences of shame and humiliation.

Repression sets up a conflict between heart and belly. When the conscious mind consistently refuses to acknowledge gut feelings—whether they be anger, sexual excitement, or fear—the outcome is physical and mental anaesthesia. Physical movements and sensations are suppressed, and numb areas develop in the body—places that seem hard and immovable, places that seem to stifle vocal resonance. Mentally, our awareness of certain emotions is dulled and very painful memories may be completely obliterated. Thus, loss of body-consciousness and emotional self-estrangement are related.

As you begin to move consciously and mindfully, know that you are stirring up the pot: anger, despair, fear, and sexuality may rise to the surface and ask to be accepted and integrated. In working with pelvic movement, both slowing down and breathing are of great importance. It is very easy to move the pelvis yet feel nothing. The outer groups of large muscles may be working while the inner musculature is tightly clinched. At a workshop in which we focused on pelvic movement, one woman asked in amazement: "How is it that I have given birth to four children yet this is the first time I ever allowed myself to really feel my genitals?" Allow yourself to explore small, gentle movements, and see if you can allow movement not only on the surface of your body but deep within. Try humming and singing as you move, and remember to *breathe!*

Meeting the Demons

Gut feelings often seem monstrously powerful and dangerous as they erupt—and yet to face them is an essential part of the hero's or the heroine's journey. When decades of repressed emotions begin to appear on the horizon, they resemble dark storms with no end in sight. I cannot recall how many times people have expressed the fear to me that if unleashed, their rage will destroy everything in sight, their despair will plunge them into an endless abyss, their tears, once freed, will not cease. It is my experience, however, that whatever the depth of the wound, it has limits, and healing is possible.

A European fairy tale tells the story of a beautiful princess who has the bad fortune to become betrothed to a hideous serpent-monster.[1] Terrified, she seeks the counsel of a wise old witch. The witch tells the princess to wear ten white shifts on her wedding night. With each garment she takes off, she is to insist that the serpent shed one of his skins as well. But after taking off her last shift, she is told that she must embrace the slimy, repulsive creature. Disgusted as she is, she nonetheless has the wisdom to carefully follow the witch's instructions, and as she embraces the serpent he miraculously transforms into her princely lover.

This story tells us precisely how to handle our inner demons. The princess completes three significant steps: she acknowledges the monster as her bridegroom, she undresses for him, and finally she embraces him. We too must face our demons—repulsive as they may seem—and accept them as our responsibility. Like the princess, we are indeed wedded to these demons, for they are an inseparable part of ourselves. Our own fear of them is the primary source of their dark power, enabling them to lurk in the dark, terrifying us. Our entire fearful world changes when we find the courage to face them, illuminating them with our awareness.

Like the princess, we must also be willing to become vulnerable in their presence. There is always a leap of faith required in letting go and entering a powerful and unknown emotional vortex. Only the act of relinquishing our defenses—the shedding of the princess's last shift—and returning to a state of innocent vulnerability will give us the power to transform our inner demons. Finally we need to embrace the monster, for only by embracing him can we release him from his ugly form. We must find the power to open our heart to what initially seems most repulsive and unlovable within ourselves.

Anger

Next to sexuality, anger is the most commonly repressed gut feeling. Spiritual aspirants are often encouraged to behave in a cooperative, non-confronting fashion, while anger is deplored as an "unspiritual" state of consciousness. In this respect, religious conditioning reaffirms social conditioning, so seekers are only too eager to tuck their anger away, often hiding it even from themselves.

It would be convenient if we could maintain perfect balance in the face of threats, criticism, attack, or rejection. It would be pleasant to remain tranquil when someone snatches the parking place we wanted. Indeed it is humbling to recognize how we cling to our self-righteousness, indulging in the same forces that threaten to destroy the earth. And yet we are human beings and our unacknowledged feelings do not simply dissolve. In our interior world, time has little meaning; even fifty years after an event, unresolved anger may surface with all its original intensity. Since we *do* get angry, hiding these emotions only adds hypocrisy, guilt, shame, and loneliness to the problem—and the unrealistic ideal becomes a trap.

In physical terms, anger is just another pattern of moving energy—a strong, fast-flowing current crying out for change. In group work, the circle can provide a safe space for a person to allow belly-rage to surface—and like a thunderstorm it may leave the air vibrant and fresh. Anger need not be destructive. On the contrary, it can lead to the recognition of previously unmet needs and thus to healing. Yet anger is rarely the most basic emotion produced by emotional trauma; it usually disguises other emotions such as fear and pain. These feelings must also be fully acknowledged before forgiveness is possible. There is nothing wrong in being angry, but to make a habit of it is unhealthy and stems from a kind of emotional laziness that obstructs the transformational flow that can carry anger into fear, fear into sadness, sadness into love.

Beyond the self-centered anger arising in response to a sense of hurt, loss, or unmet need, the belly contains another energy that might be described as selfless anger. The Indian goddess Durga embodies this powerful

The Hindu mother-goddess Durga rides her lion into battle to protect her children's welfare, 18th century.

spiritual force when she appears as a warrior moving into battle to destroy the demons, her anger fueled by love for the exploited earth and the earth's suffering children. While selfish anger controls a person, Durga instead draws upon her anger as a source of wisdom guiding her toward right action. Her face appears serene and smiling as she moves into battle. Dressed in the fiery crimson of passionate love, she rides a tiger or a lion, symbolizing her ability to tame even the most ferocious energies of nature. This is the kind of anger we see in such rare beings such as Dr. Martin Luther King, Jr., or Mahatma Gandhi, in whom love, anger, and right action are one and the same.

Many of us today feel overwhelming grief and anger as we witness the destruction of earth's fragile ecology. When honored, these gut feelings can potentially liberate tremendous human energy that may be channeled toward the planet's protection. It is crucial to question the labeling of our instinct toward self-preservation as primitive, base, and selfish. Clearly, the earth's survival can only be considered a *spiritual* concern if life itself is held sacred. The Buddhist ecologist Joanna Macy, in her book *Despair and Personal Power in the Nuclear Age,* explains:

> Feelings of pain for our world are natural and healthy. Confronted
> with widespread suffering and threats of global disaster, responses of

anguish—of fear, anger, and grief and even guilt—are normal. They are a measure of our humanity. And these feelings are probably what we most have in common. Just by virtue of sharing this particular planet-time, we know these feelings more than our own grandparents or any earlier generation could have. We are in grief together. And this grief for our world cannot be reduced to private pathology. We experience it in addition to whatever personal griefs, frustrations, and neuroses we bear. Not to experience it would be a sign of intellectual and moral atrophy, but that is academic, for I have met no one who is immune to this pain.[2]

To disregard our gut feelings is to sacrifice our gut wisdom, cutting ourselves off from the passion we will need if we are to preserve our planet for future generations. It is not surprising that so many cultures associate such passionate, protective anger with the goddess and with the feminine. While patriarchy has placed great value on detachment from creation, the feminine path has regarded creation as sacred, evoking our powers of protection. As mothers and guardians of each new generation, women most naturally harness Durga's anger. Every mother embodies the warrior, whose instincts tell her to fight for the lives of her children. Yet in this century alone, enormous numbers of women have witnessed their children sent to war and butchered. Their anger and grief have been repressed and disqualified. We are expected to believe that our wars are necessary and even heroic; we blind ourselves to their insanity, perversity, and wastefulness. The deep anger we feel as we witness the rape of our planet is akin to the fury of the mother-goddess Durga. This fury also resides in our belly; we must claim it as an ally and friend.

Reclaiming the Pelvis

Spiritual teachings from many parts of the world describe an *energy body* as well as the *physical body*. Also known as the *astral* or *subtle* body, this energy body contains what in Sanskrit are called *chakras,* from the word

meaning wheel. A chakra is a spinning vortex of energy and is easily
discernable in the heightened awareness evoked through movement meditation. Because many other authors
describe the chakras and their functions in great detail, I will leave the
description of this information to
other texts.[3] The important point in
this context is that the chakras are not
separate centers of energy, but belong
to a single spectrum much as the
colors of the rainbow emerge out of
white light. Earlier, we discussed the

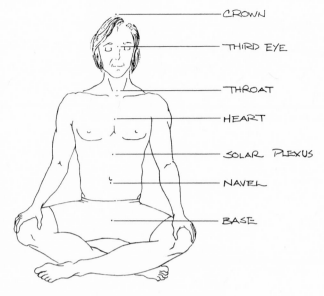

concept of reality as a single spectrum ranging from visible, tangible matter
through increasingly more subtle manifestations of energy to invisible, immeasurably subtle spirit. A graph of this spectrum could be overlaid upon
the image of the human spine: the lower chakras correspond to our ways
of relating to physical existence, while the upper chakras are concerned
with our experience of the most subtle realms of spiritual manifestation.

As mentioned previously, Western civilization has tended to disregard
the continuous nature of the spectrum of consciousness, segregating matter
from spirit, body from soul. This division has resulted in a fragmentation
of the body itself, which has been cut in two. We have come to consider the
upper body, with its reasoning faculties, the more noble and valuable half,
while the lower body and all its functions have been heavily burdened with
shame. If we observe a typical group of Westerners in motion, we notice
that many bodies appear to have been cut off from the waist downwards.
No wonder we are disconnected from our gut wisdom.

Patriarchal religions based on dualistic doctrine describe human spiritual evolution as a movement out of the "base" lower body into the upper
body. Such concepts prevent us from remaining in contact with gut feelings,
however, and foster the kind of hypocrisy embodied by the religious leader
who publicly upholds the strictest moral values yet in private has seedy af-

fairs. In Western medical terminology, we still speak of the base of the spinal column as the sacrum—from the Latin *os sacrum,* the sacred bone— but we are not raised to think of our pelvic areas as sacred.

The Japanese concept of Hara supports a more holistic image of evo- lutionary development. Hara is like the centerpoint of a circle. No matter how much the circumference of a circle expands, its center point does not budge. In the same way, Hara remains the center of our physical and spir- itual being throughout life. When a potter throws her clay on the wheel, the clay must be centered before it can ever be formed into a vessel. If im- properly centered, the pot's walls will break as the opening widens. Spiri- tual evolution then could be described as the process of becoming firmly settled in one's center.

The Buddha, representative of the enlightened human being, is often portrayed with a round belly, symbolizing his power to protect, his healing wisdom, and nurturing compassion for all beings. A buddha is a man or woman utterly centered in gut wisdom, in whom the vital energy of the Hara manifests only as loving compassion, and who uses the power of the Hara not to dominate others but to serve them in creative and compassion- ate ways.

A Serpent Dream

If we deny or repress our gut feelings, the power of the serpentine energy within us is stifled. Some years ago, I was suffering from a serious and per- sistent pelvic inflammation. After asking my inner guidance for a healing dream, I dreamed the following:

> At a university I am visiting, I am being shown around. I am taken to a room where students are rehearsing for a ritual drama they plan to enact.
>
> Entering the room, I see an eighty-foot-long snake lying on the ground. A kind of wooden casing encloses the lower part of its body. I am told that during the ritual the snake must free itself by emerging from its confinement. A man standing next to the serpent is to play the

role of a demon who will try to prevent the snake from liberating itself. But the man appears dull-witted, and so the snake's ultimate victory is certain.

I witness the rehearsal. The snake first attempts to burn its wooden casing off by setting it on fire. The man counters by sawing away the burning portion of the casing. But because he is dull-witted, he does not cut away enough and the fire is not fully extinguished; glowing embers remain. I gaze at the serpent with admiration. It is enormous, and out the top of its head brilliant white light bursts forth like a crown. I awake flooded with great joy.

This dream reassured me I would be healed; my inner serpent would certainly free itself. I began to see the infection in a new light—not only as a symptom of disease, but as one of the weapons my own serpentine energy had wielded against some form of constriction. Through the inflammation, it was trying to burn its way to freedom. The demon, in his ignorance, reminded me of my doctor's heavy-handed yet unsuccessful attempts to suppress the infection with increasingly large doses of antibiotics that merely depleted my immune system. The process of healing began as I rejected further antibiotic treatment and took responsibility for my body, consciously following the guidance of my intuition.

At a deeper level, I recognize in the demon the repressive messages of my upbringing that have instructed me, as a woman, how I may and may not use my sexual energies. Internalized, these voices tell me freedom is unsafe and that I must contain my energies, causing my body to develop a hard casing of fear and vigilance deep inside my pelvis. Though overwhelmingly strong, the demon is also stupid—a regressive creature of the past. As the serpent dances her way out, there is nothing he can do to stop her.

Developing Fluid Boundaries

If we compare the human being to a circle, then Hara represents the center. Its circumference on the other hand is defined by the ego, our internal capacity that defines and defends our personal boundaries. The ego could be described as a border-patrol, or a limit-setter. Since the body is defined by its boundaries, our ego determines how we inhabit and use our bodies. A healthy ego can erect strong boundaries: we know how much space, physically and psychically, we need for ourselves, and we can respect others' boundaries as well.

Boundaries are an important function of physical survival. When the skin, the boundary of the physical body, is injured, pain immediately alerts our organism to the presence of danger and the need for self-protective action. Yet, unfortunately, the term *ego* has become a dirty word, a synonym for immaturity and selfishness. It is almost as if the ego, in current spiritual jargon, has taken the place the devil once occupied; whatever obstructs our enlightenment is blamed on the ego. Since the ego functions primarily through the lower chakras, the expression of gut feelings is often considered "egoistic" or "selfish," further reinforcing our tendency to devalue the pelvic area. When a person's boundaries dissolve and she has no ability to establish them, however, the result is not enlightenment but psychosis.

We must clearly understand that the ego is not a physical or even a mental entity. The ego is neither a person nor a "thing" but rather a pattern: a tendency to think, feel, and act in certain ways. Like all habits, the ego fluctuates. The ego can both support and sabotage our spiritual evolution; instead of judging it as the adversary of the enlightened state, we should recognize in it our potentially strongest ally in spiritual awakening.

Notice how much space you claim for yourself. Can you say "no" without feeling guilty, and can you hold your boundaries in a powerful and grounded way? Can you maintain your separateness when it is appropriate, or do you automatically merge with others to the point of self-betrayal?

Once, as I was walking through a city park, a strange man approached and grabbed me, clearly intent on raping me. Responding to pure instinct, I kicked him hard in the stomach and ran as fast as I could. Today, I still feel proud of how I protected myself. Though this is an extreme example of an invasion of boundaries, it reminds us that our sense of spirituality should not include letting ourselves be mistreated in any way. Whenever we allow ourselves to be abused, we lose our center by participating in loveless action.

The ability to establish and maintain boundaries, however, must be offset by the equally important ability to remain open to intimacy and closeness. A healthy ego will allow boundaries to pulsate and shift—even, at times, to dissolve entirely—since it is able to recognize and surrender to love. As the spiritual guide Emmanuel says, "True intelligence is the capacity of the mind to honor the wisdom of the heart."[4] Without expansion of boundaries, neither sexual nor spiritual lovemaking are possible. Prayer, for example, is essentially an opening of one's boundaries to invite guidance and help from higher sources. One cannot pray without allowing the expansion of ego-boundaries. Similarly, movement meditation invites an opening of one's entire being to the universe.

The importance of developing a healthy ego, an ego able to both create and dissolve boundaries, cannot be emphasized enough. During the past decade I have led many women's retreats and am accustomed to receiving calls afterward from distressed women who did not realize how difficult the transition back to "normal" life was going to be. Returning to a family or work situation where openheartedness is not supported and perhaps even discouraged, we may feel frustrated and angry at the outside world that seems bent on destroying our previous bliss and dragging us into regressive patterns. When we expand psychically, we may find that a previously comfortable situation now feels like a tight shoe. Like a fragile young plant that still needs protection, we need to find teachers and others in the community who can support us through the process of our new growth.

A healthy ego is the essential basis for expanding into higher forms of consciousness. All intensive meditation practices encourage the expansion or dissolution of ego boundaries, and yet, in order to function in everyday life, we need to reestablish these boundaries. It is impossible to swing back and forth between the demands of modern life and the unbounded space of deep meditative experience without having cultivated a high degree of ego flexibility. For this reason, Eastern spiritual traditions consider the practice of centering in the belly so fundamental. If the center does not hold firm, severe mental distress may occur, as is not uncommon with people who enter intensive meditation programs without adequate preparation. But if the center is solid, then—like a clay vessel being formed—the boundaries can expand and contract without harm.

The practice of centering in your belly will help you develop boundaries that can shift easily and effortlessly at a moment's notice. Your centeredness will enable you to respond appropriately and with integrity to any situation.

CHAPTER FIVE: MEDITATIONS

Exercises for the Pelvis and the Spine

RECOMMENDED MUSIC: Meditation music or rhythmic music

The following exercises will help you loosen up your spine and pelvis, improving your balance and grounding. They also make great warm-ups. Loosening your pelvis and increasing its mobility prepares your body so that it can translate inner experience into the language of movement.

The German word for pelvis is *Becken,* which literally translates as bowl. This term aptly describes this part of the our body. As a bowl resting on the two pillars of your legs, the pelvis can only rotate as far as your legs allow. If your knees are straight and locked into place, you cannot move your pelvis at all. Therefore a ground rule is that you must keep your feet slightly apart and your knees bent to allow mobility in the pelvis. Of course this means hard work for the thighs. If you find that your legs are not strong enough to support you for very long, just shake them out, give them a rest, and start again.

Floor Exercises

Lie down on your back. Place one hand on your abdomen, about two inches below the navel. Breathe deeply. Feel your abdomen rising and falling beneath your hand. Notice the sensations in your belly— warmth, spaciousness, tension, excitement.

Observe your breath carefully.

Begin to tilt your pelvis very slightly. Move it in any direction you want, and then release it again. Tilt it to one side, then to the other, and let it go. Breathe.

Tilt upward, pressing the small of your back against the floor. Let go. Tilt downward, increasing the arch of your spine, and let go.

Move your pelvis in all directions. Make sure there is no tensing around your genitals or anus. All the time, watch your breath. If you notice that you have stopped breathing, see if you can repeat the same movement without holding. Let your breath flow easily through you, like water, and allow your pelvis, too, to become like water: fluid and soft in its motions.

Continue until the breath and the movement flow into each other without interference—both utterly soft, fluid, and effortless—two rivers intermingling in your belly.

Allow the movements to ripple from your belly into the rest of your body. Let go of efforting, let go of your will. Just watch, and breathe. If something wants to ripple outward, undulate through you, let it happen. If there is just breath and stillness, that is fine too.

Stay focused on the sensations in your belly. Let everything emanate from that center, and let your whole body be as soft and fluid as water, moved gently by the breath.

Then just lie in silence for a minute or two.

Sideways Tilting

Stand in the basic grounded position with your knees slightly bent. Slowly tilt your pelvis from one side to another and back. Try to do this without shifting your weight from one leg to the other. Your weight remains equally balanced over both legs.

Make sure you keep breathing and do not tighten your belly, anus, or genital area while moving. The entire pelvis should stay relaxed.

Notice how your pelvis relates to your chest and shoulders. If you tilt your hips from side to side, do your shoulders remain still? Or do they move too? There is no right or wrong here, just notice what is going on while you move. Try both possibilities.

Notice that your pelvic movement seems to outline the shape of a bowl. As you move, breathe through the bowl of your pelvis. Let your mind, too, be an empty bowl, receptive, listening, and present.

Spinal Arches

Spinal arching is a very important exercise. It involves the whole body, and the different positions correspond to different mental states.

Often, our own body image is distorted, and we are not moving as we think we are. If possible, do this exercise in front of a mirror at first. Observe your posture very carefully, comparing it with the illustrations.

Begin by standing with your feet about ten inches apart, knees bent. First, try tilting your pelvis forward. This corresponds to the movement of flattening out the small of your back. You can also try flattening your back against a wall. You should feel as if you are "tucking your tail"; push your pubic bone forward as much as possible, lengthening your back.

Now slowly lift your arms. Imagine yourself hugging a giant ball pressed against your body. Let your head drop slightly. Your entire spine should be slightly curled inward.

Now tilt your pelvis backward, arching your whole spine. The shoulders and the head will fall back slightly. Look at yourself from the side in the mirror, and compare what you see with the illustration below. If you have found the correct position, you will feel quite grounded. Someone in this position is not easily pushed over. This is a position of openness, with the front of the body completely exposed—still, the balance of the entire body is maintained. If the first position was one of introversion, this is one of extroversion, of coming out versus going in. But neither withdrawing nor opening will feel safe unless we are balanced and centered in ourselves.

It is important that your body remain balanced. Some people give up their balance by leaning backward while pushing their pelvis forward. This position is very stressful to the jaws, neck, and back. Others give up their balance by leaning forward. Look at your spine from the side and see whether it is balanced.

If you notice that you have a tendency to go off balance, consider what the off-balance position does for you, what purpose it serves, and why you have adopted it. The centered position is a position of power, but also of self-protection—the entire vulnerable front of the body is protected. Some people fear that they will be pushed forward from behind, and thus they lean back in resistance, even when the pushy mother, father, or authority figure is no longer present. Others hunch their shoulders as if in fear of a blow from above. Our whole history is written in the stance we take.

Once you have found the two basic positions, begin to alternate between them, moving very slowly. Gently, arch your spine in both directions. Remember to keep your knees bent, and shake out your legs when they get tired. As you alternate, breathe, and notice the different feeling states that accompany each position.

As you move, you are like a flower, which opens into the sunlight, and closes gently as the sun goes down. There is a natural rhythm to this cycle; it is a rhythm that flows through all aspects of your life— through the daily activities, your relationships, and your work.

Spinal Waves

As you become familiar with spinal arches, you may find them naturally developing into serpentine undulations. Spinal waves gently release tension all along the spine, increasing flexibility and realigning the vertebrae. Serpentine movements will also help minimize scoliosis.

Again, your spine alternates between a fully arched, expanded position, and a fully contracted, curled-up one. But the switch occurs not all at once, but rather in a slow wave that begins at the base of your spine and travels all the way up to the top of your head. It is as if the message to change positions were not reaching your entire spine at once, but instead traveling slowly from the base upwards.

First, push your pelvis forward, tucking your tail. Then, let the impulse of this movement travel upward. The wave reaches your heart and shoulders, curling them forward, and finally, your neck and head follow. You are now in the contracted or closed position.

Again, the wave begins from the base of the spine, but this time you are opening your spine into the arched position. From its base, the movement flows upward until, last of all, your head falls back and your face turns gently to the sky.

Try to visualize a continuous flow of waves up your spine. Just as ocean waves overlap, so you too may find the waves of movement in your body overlapping, the next wave beginning before the first one ends.

Please don't be discouraged if you find these movements difficult. Simply imagine how they would look and feel. Even if you think you cannot do the spinal waves, one day as you dance, you may suddenly find yourself doing them quite effortlessly.

The following is a stylized diagram of the various positions the spine moves through in the course of one single wave motion. The dot indicates the position of the movement impulse:

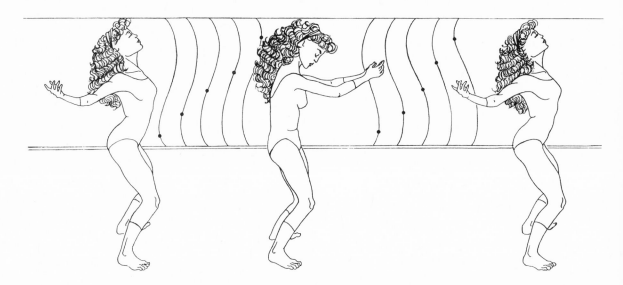

Another basic spinal wave movement is created by arching the spine to the right and left, instead of backward and forward. The same diagram of the wave movement traveling up the spine applies to this movement.

Pelvic Circles

In circling the pelvis, one direction (usually counterclockwise) invariably feels easier than the other. Be sure to practice both directions. Maintain a balanced position throughout your body. The pelvic circle combines the side-to-side tilt and the front-to-back tilt.

Begin at the right side. Very slowly, start to circle around to the front, the left, the back, returning to the right. Move slowly, and remember to breathe.

Note that in this exercise you are isolating the pelvis from the upper torso. *Do not shift your weight from side to side, and try not to move your upper body.* While your pelvis circles, your upper body remains as still as possible. It can be helpful to place a hand on your heart as you practice the pelvic circles and feel it resting quietly, moved only by the flow of your breath.

Close your eyes and continue to circle very slowly, trying to make your circles as smooth and round as possible. Begin to visualize the circles as you move, as if you were painting them with your pelvis. Try to experience exactly where in your belly the center is and visualize it as a bright red dot or point of light. As you circle, remember to breathe gently through your center. Make sure that your whole body, especially your neck and shoulders, remains relaxed the whole time, and that you don't hold your breath.

When you get tired, stretch and shake out your legs. Then repeat the circling in the opposite direction.

Because the body moves in three dimensions, we can draw circles with our pelvis along three basic planes. The easiest way to visualize these three planes is to face the wall of any room. The first plane is the horizontal one, which could be represented by a circle painted on the floor. So far, you have been moving with this horizontal circle.

Now imagine a circle on the wall facing you: this is the second plane. In order to draw this circle with your pelvis, you must combine an up-and-down movement (bending and straightening your knees) with a side-to-side movement, which involves both a sideways tilting of the pelvis, and a shifting of the weight from one leg to another.

Finally, imagine the third circle painted on the wall that runs alongside you. You can draw this circle by combining an up-and-down movement with a forward and backward tilting of the spine.

Pelvic Spirals and Figure Eights

Spiral movements help you to focus on your navel center and experience it as the end or beginning point of your spiral. If your pelvis is still quite rigid or you have any difficulty at all with the pelvic circles, however, you may find spirals rather difficult. Using the same technique as in the pelvic circles, try drawing the following spiral designs with your pelvis.

For figure eights, assume the same starting position as for the pelvic circles: feet shoulder-width apart, knees bent. Try to draw a flat, horizontal figure eight with your pelvis. Imagine that the figure eight is drawn on the floor: two circles, side by side, one surrounding each of your feet.

To start, shift your weight onto your left foot, and draw a pelvic circle starting from the right to the back, the left, the front, and again to the right. Now let your weight shift onto the right foot and draw a second circle, moving in the opposite direction: from the left to the back, right, front left. Shift back onto the left leg and repeat. Gradually let your movements become flowing and easy.

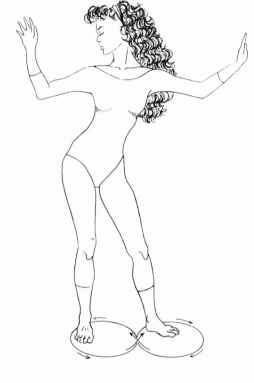

This illustration shows one of the variations of the pelvic spiral that you can do to loosen your pelvis. You might also try rotating the figure eights so that they are no longer horizontal as if drawn on the floor beneath your feet, but vertical as if painted on the wall facing you.

Axis Mundi

RECOMMENDED MUSIC: Silence or meditation music

The religious historian Mircea Eliade, in his book *The Sacred & The Profane,* writes at length about the symbology of the *axis mundi,* the world axis or central pillar, which supports all that exists. This central pillar may be represented by a tree, a sanctuary located at the center of the world, a sacred mountain, or a temple replicating the sacred mountain. As examples of such holy mountains, Eliade cites Mount Meru in India, Haraberezaiti in Iran, the mythical Mount of the Lands in Mesopotamia, and Gerizin in Palestine. The same principle of centrality determines how native people arrange their villages and houses; for a native American, the centerpole of her tipi symbolizes the axis mundi, the spiritual as well as the physical center of existence. Eliade describes:

> . . . religious man's will to take his stand at the very heart of the real, at the Center of the World—that is, exactly where the cosmos came into existence and began to spread out toward the four horizons, and where, too, there is the possibility of communication with the gods; in short, precisely where he is *closest to the gods.*[5]

The universal image of the central pillar undoubtedly originates in the human body, with the spinal column as its central pillar of support. Thus, in movement meditation, the spine is the primary focus of attention, not the arms and legs, as in Western dance. The point in which the central pillar is believed to emerge from the earth's surface is often called "the navel of the universe," which corresponds to the fact that, in movement meditation, centering in the spinal column and centering in the navel take place simultaneously.

The following meditation introduces you into the experience of your own body as the axis mundi. Since Step Three will include the pelvic circle, refer to page 111 for a description of the pelvic circle and make sure you are comfortable with it before moving on to Step Three. Otherwise, conclude with Step Two.

Step One

} Stand, with your feet at about shoulder-width apart. Close your eyes. Visualize the axis of the universe as it runs from the center of the earth up through your body into the sky. Now try the following pattern of breath and movement:

Breath	Movement	Mind
Exhale	Keeping your spine balanced, allow your knees to bend slightly with the exhalation.	Let your awareness drop out of the sky down into your head, through your spine and through the soles of your feet downward into the earth.
Inhale Exhale Inhale Exhale Inhale Exhale	Remain in the same position with bent knees. Make sure your neck and shoulders stay relaxed.	*Focus on your exhalations* and as you exhale, let your awareness drop down to the very center of the earth. Exhaling, drop into the moist darkness, down through the rock into the glowing, fiery core of the planet.
Inhale	Straighten your legs.	Let your spirit soar upward, bursting through the surface of the earth into your feet, rushing upward through your body, through your head, and out the top of your head into space.
Exhale Inhale Exhale Inhale Exhale Inhale	Remain standing.	*Focus on your inhalations.* Soar up, into the light of the sky, inhaling light, bathing your whole body in light. Merge with the radiance of clear light.

} Repeat this until you feel that the flow of energy through your spine, both upward and downward, is established.

Step Two

{ Continue to breathe and move according to the same pattern as before, but now moving back and forth between your navel and your heart center.

Breath	Movement	Mind
Exhale	Bend your knees.	Exhaling, gently float down into the navel center, approximately two inches below the navel. Here, all the radiant heat of the earth's core is gathered, a great storehouse of energy.
Inhale Exhale Inhale Exhale Inhale	Remain in the same position with bent knees.	*Focus on your exhalations* and on your navel center. Feel your navel connected to the earth's center. Visualize a glowing red light in your navel center, and feel the warmth and the sense of nourishment and well-being it radiates through your body.
Inhale	Straighten your legs.	Let your spirit float up gently into your heart center in the center of your chest. See your spirit settling into your heart as gently as a dove landing in a tree.
Exhale Inhale Exhale Inhale Exhale Inhale	Remain standing.	*Focus on your inhalations.* Breathe through your heart, visualizing it as a rich, golden glow that radiates love and a sense of abundance through you. Feel your heart as one with the infinite space above.

Step Three

} Continue with the same pattern of breath and movement. Only now, while you are standing with bent knees doing three cycles of inhalations and exhalations, add three pelvic circles moving counterclockwise. Try to visualize the circles as you move.

Breath	Movement	Mind
Exhale	Bend your knees.	Exhaling, gently float down into the navel center, approximately two inches below the navel. Here, all the radiant heat of the earth's core is gathered, an infinite supply of energy.
Inhale Exhale Inhale Exhale Inhale Exhale	Remain in the same position with bent knees.	*Focus on your exhalations* and on your navel center. Feel your navel connected to the earth's center. Visualize a glowing red light in your navel center. Moving in a counterclockwise direction, draw three pelvic circles. Try to see these circles as you move.
Inhale	Straighten your legs.	Let your spirit float up gently into your heart center, in the center of your chest. See your spirit settling into your heart as gently as a dove landing in a tree.
Exhale Inhale Exhale Inhale Exhale Inhale	Remain standing.	*Focus on your inhalations.* Breathe through your heart, visualizing it as a rich, golden glow that radiates love and a sense of abundance through you. Feel your heart as one with the infinite space above.

} Repeat this sequence for several more minutes.

CHAPTER SIX

Befriending the Snake

In India, even the most poisonous snake, the cobra, is a sacred animal, and the mythological Serpent King is the next thing to the Buddha. The serpent represents the power of life engaged in the field of time, and of death, yet eternally alive. The world is but its shadow—the falling skin.

The serpent was revered in the American Indian traditions, too. The serpent was thought of as a very important power to be made friends with. Go down to the pueblos, for example, and watch the snake dance of the Hopi, where they take the snakes in their mouths and make friends with them and then send them back to the hills. The snakes are sent back to carry the human message to the hills, just as they have brought the message of the hills to the humans. The interplay of man and nature is illustrated in this relationship with the serpent.

JOSEPH CAMPBELL

Remembering the Body's Serpentine Movements

INNUMERABLE MYTHS from Europe, the Middle East, Asia, Africa, and the Americas associate serpents with everything most sacred and essential to human life: the cycle of birth and death, the mystery of sex, the interwoven trinity of health, wholeness, and holiness. To this day, the serpent is worshipped in many parts of the world as an emblem of divinity. A well-known example is the Snake Dance by which the Hopi of the Southwestern United States invoke the rain. Throughout Africa snakes are venerated, and in Southern India many shrines are dedicated to the *nagas,* the serpent-deities.

As our ancestors watched the snake emerging from the husk of an old skin, as if reborn, perhaps they heard it whisper, "Behold the cycle of life and death and rebirth. As the year turns from winter to spring, so am I renewed, and so you also shall leave behind the old shell of your body and be reborn." As they watched it slithering through the grass, it told them, "I am that which is neither right nor left, neither good nor evil, but two in one." And when they began to explore the secrets of its venom, its life-giving and its lethal properties, it said, "Within me I contain that which brings life and that which summons death—and they are not separate but one."

Through movement meditation we rediscover our relationship with the serpent and the wave. Considering the central role that serpent and wave imagery plays in so many spiritual traditions, it is not surprising to find that people in all parts of the world have played with the serpent-waves of their own moving bodies and have become fascinated by the ability of wave movements to entrance and harmonize the psyche. In the body's rippling, trembling, pulsating, undulating motions, they discovered a natural inroad into ecstasy.

As the rational mind relinquishes its control, we cross over into the fluid, serpentine realm of swirling energy currents, an enterprise requiring humility, courage, skill, and reverence. Any encounter with the serpentine energies is a step into unknown territory outside the ego's jurisdiction, a journey crossing the borderlands between our everyday reality and the great beyond. In many societies, this crossing was guided by a shaman who knew the way. Sacred dance and movement are among the most ancient and powerful shamanic practices of crossing over, of leaving behind the realm of everyday consciousness and entering the domain of the serpent.

The body's serpentine movements are nonlinear, involving the complex interaction of hundreds of muscles. In no way can the mind comprehend their complexity and speed. Paradoxically, these movements do not feel complicated but, on the contrary, absolutely natural and pleasurable. Wave movements appear spontaneously in our dance when we are relaxed, at peace with ourselves, and at one with the innocence of our bodies. From walking to lovemaking and childbirth—all the truly primal body movements are wave movements; to dance with them is to touch upon the body's deepest wisdom. These rhythmic undulations provide the essential prerequisite for the experience of being at home in one's body; they are our primary connection to the nurturing harmony within the universe. Wave movements calm the unconscious as the rocking of the cradle soothes an infant.

To lose these primal wave and serpentine movements is to become an alien in one's own body. Unfortunately, body knowledge is neither taught nor valued in the Western educational system. This is the problem in many dance classes: those who are dissociated from the primary wave motions of their body—and this is probably the majority—struggle to learn all kinds of complex movements but have never learned the most basic ways of riding the waves of their body. Highly educated people are often those most out of touch with their internal wave movements; their specialized linear mental skills are of little value here. Understandably, they often become frustrated and give up dancing. But long-forgotten wave movements *can* be remembered through the patient practice of simple, repetitive movements. When you come into harmony with your body, there is a great sense of relief; body, emotions, mind, and spirit become peaceful and balanced.

The Snake within the Body

"The Tao begot one. One begot two. Two begot three. And three begot the ten thousand things," says the ancient Chinese text Tao Te Ching.[1] Creation is movement: as the one divides in two, an alternating rhythm begins to pulsate between the polarities, exciting the first wave motion into being. This primordial wave manifests as sound, light, rhythm, and matter; developing consciousness, it appears in the form of a snake. For what is a snake other than a single undulating, pulsating wave-motion? In terms of evolutionary history, the snake is one of the oldest creatures on earth, but far more ancient even than its physical form is the wave principle it embodies, a living link to the beginning of time and to that which is primal, primitive, and unthinkably ancient within us.

Waves form in the play of wind, water, sand; in the slow dances of mountains; and in fields of grass rippling in the breeze. Though in higher forms of evolution, the primal wave may disguise itself within more complex movements, it nonetheless remains the basic pattern of all moving energy. Watch a squirrel as it jumps, a single wave from nose to tail. Observe the leap of deer, the rippling body of fish, the sinuous leopard as stalking prey, and you will see the wave motion.

Where, then, does the snake-wave appear within the human being? It dwells, first and foremost, within our very center, the spine, which, viewed from the side, looks like a snake, and moves like a snake. Further, it presides over the entire underworld of the body, governing many of our involuntary movements: the swallowing of food, the pulsating flow of blood, the peristaltic movement of the intestines, the pulsating rhythm of orgasm, and the tiny undulations that ripple through muscle tissue. The snake symbolizes everything within our bodies and minds that moves under the surface, hidden from the light of consciousness. Through the practice of movement meditation, we seek alignment with the serpentine forces by utilizing duality as a gateway into the consciousness of at-oneness.

In sacred dance, the serpent is expressed and honored in a full, conscious way. All parts of the body join in a sinuous, sensual flow of grace and

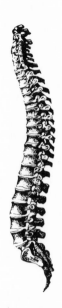

The serpentine nature of the spinal column appears clearly in the side view.

power, aligning and harmonizing the voluntary and involuntary functions of the body. And because involuntary body movements are the physical correlative of the unconscious, in working with the serpentine movements we are also aligning our conscious mind with the unconscious psychic forces. This alignment, when it is deep and complete, will produce altered states of consciousness and profound ecstasy.

Serpentine Mythology

Guardian of the jewel of enlightenment hidden within the material world, the snake has long been regarded as a representative of divinity. To this day, the people of India express their reverence toward the serpentine forces, both within and without, by erecting small "snakestones" near the temples, where they leave offerings of milk for the cobras living nearby. Often, serpents appear in conjunction with the Great Goddess, symbolizing her dominion over the primal wave energies of creation. Not only is she accompanied by her serpents or adorned with them, but they may also emerge out

Shakti, the creative serpentine force, emerging from a woman's vulva. Southern India, circa 1800 C.E.

of her vagina, reflecting her role as sexual initiator and as mother of all beings. In *Lady of the Beasts,* painter Buffie Johnson cites examples of snake worship in prehistoric cultures from Egypt and the Middle East, Crete, Greece, North and South America, Japan, China, India, Scandinavia, Africa, and Australia.[2]

Yet it is important to keep in mind that serpentine energy, like all primal nature forces, is neither inherently masculine nor feminine: serpents also coil around the neck and waist of Shiva Nataraja, Lord of the Dance, and stream from his flying hair. In one hand he holds a drum, in the other fire—symbols of sound and light, the two primary wave energies of creation. Vishnu, another great representation of god in Hindu religion, holds a conch and a disk, once again symbolizing sound and light, as he reclines on the cosmic serpent Shesha, a huge, many-headed cobra. The Babylonian god Pazazu is named "he of the serpent penis,"[3] and other innumerable deities are associated with serpents. It would be a mistake to interpret the serpent solely as a symbol of femininity, or to identify the snake with one or the other gender. Serpents represent, above all, the balance of all polarities:

male and female in harmony, matter and spirit united, light as both particle and wave, infinity contained within the finite.

It is said that after the snake-haired Medusa was beheaded, Asklepius, the Greek god of healing, "secured the blood from the veins of Medusa, both from her left side and from her right. With the former he slays, but with the latter he cures and brings back to life."[4] Not only can the venom of the serpent both kill and heal, but everything about the snake speaks of the union of opposites. Shedding its skin, it reenacts the cyclical mysteries of nature: death and rebirth, the seasons, the cycles of the waxing and waning moon. Above all, its undulating movement implies the ambiguity of what cannot be grasped in a linear way. Like the serpent, the energy that impels spiritual evolution moves not in a linear fashion, but in oscillating waves, hastened by the creative tension between the polar opposites of man and woman, matter and spirit.

Symbolizing the oneness of opposites, serpents appear in the context of the most primitive, unevolved life forms, and also in conjunction with the highest manifestations of enlightened consciousness. They are the sacred attributes of gods and goddesses, but they also inhabit the underworld and the dark terrain of the primitive and unconscious realms. Ambiguous in every sense, serpent power is the power of primeval nature itself: inherently neither good nor bad. Like electricity, another manifestation of wave energy, snake power has equal creative and destructive potential. Indeed, according to the present-day Hopi Indians, serpent power and electricity are one and the same, for they say that the snake goes deep within the earth mother to tap the powerful electromagnetic fields created by the earth's rotation, by which it becomes a master of vibrational energy.

In many myths the serpents themselves are paired, as they are in the twisted caduceus symbol adopted by the medical profession. Joseph Campbell, the ground-breaking scholar and teacher of mythology, retells the wonderful Greek myth of how the blind prophet Tiresias unwittingly stumbled onto the serpent's mysteries:

> Tiresias offended with a stroke of his stick two immense serpents, mating, and (O wonder!) was changed from man to woman. Thus he lived

for seven years. In the eighth, he saw the same two again and said: "If in striking you there be such virtue that the doer of the deed is changed into his opposite, then I shall now strike once more"; which he did, and his former shape returned, so that again he had the gender of his birth.[5]

Campbell's comments on this story are particularly revealing:

> In this tale the mating serpents, like those of the caduceus, are the sign of the world-generating force that plays through all pairs of opposites, male and female, birth and death. Into their mystery Tiresias blundered as he wandered in the green wood of the secrets of the ever-living goddess Earth. His impulsive stroke placed him between the two, like the middle staff *(axis mundi)* . . . and he was thereupon flashed to the other side for seven years—a week of years, a little life—the side of which he formerly had had no knowledge. Whence, with intent, he again touched the living symbol of the two that are in nature one, and returning to his proper form, was thereafter the one who was in knowledge both: in wisdom greater than either Zeus, the god who was merely male, or his goddess, who was merely female.
>
> The patriarchal point of view is distinguished from the earlier archaic view by its setting apart of all pairs of opposites—male and female, life and death, true and false, good and evil—as though they were absolutes in themselves and not merely aspects of the larger entity of life.[6]

The Cursing of the Serpent

Like the stratified rock of an ancient canyon, biblical mythology is many-layered: some layers bear witness to the older pre-patriarchal era, while others reflect a later reversal of cultural values. Both Jehovah and Jesus were originally associated with the serpent. In one example from the Old Testament, Moses receives a sign of authorization from God: the prophet's staff, thrown upon the ground, becomes a snake. As Moses backs away from it in fear, God orders him to seize the snake by its tail. Just as Moses grasps the creature, it transforms back into a staff. Once again, like the staff of the Greek god Asklepius, Moses' staff contains within it a living power that the Hindus call *Shakti;* its undulating, oscillating waves of energy reveal themselves to those able to discern the serpentine dance beneath the surface of solid matter.

Merlin Stone notes that the biblical story of the Garden of Eden derives from earlier myths, in which the great Mother Goddess appears as a serpent.[7] Hers is the Garden, hers the tree, originally known as the Tree of Life; the knowledge she offers the initiate is the knowledge not only of good and evil, but of all the dualities that define embodied existence. Indeed, many of our stories about the downfall of an evil dragon may well have a concrete historical reference point in the overthrow of matriarchy. Because the serpent was identified with the Goddess, the account of this deadly creature of evil meeting its death may reflect the patriarchal rulers' view of their own takeover as the victory of good over evil. In fact, it also marks the tragic eradication of the concepts of wholeness and duality from Western consciousness.

With the advent of a single heavenly, transcendent god, the wisdom of the earthbound serpent-deity is rejected, and the serpent's androgynous nature is denied in favor of its exclusive association with the feminine. Adam and Eve, however, obey the serpent; rejecting their previous state of transcendence, they embark on the path of immanence and conscious embodiment. From the perspective of the transcendent father-god, their entrance into the realm and experience of duality is seen as a fall from grace, and so, the wrathful patriarch proceeds to punish his children. Eve's disobedience is particularly offensive as it reflects her allegiance to the serpentine forces. In later centuries, Christian clerics forbade women from teaching the scriptures based on 1 Timothy 2:14, which refers to Eve's offense: "Adam was not deceived, but the woman was deceived and became a transgressor." The serpent becomes the only one of God's creatures to be cursed by its own creator and is now exclusively associated with woman. She is henceforth punished for her loyalty to the goddess-principle by her subjugation to man's dominion. Indeed, there is a certain irony to the fact that the snake, symbol of nature's instinctual energies, should be punished by having to crawl with its belly on the earth; after all, it was the serpent's closeness to the earth that originally inspired human beings to worship it.

Having cursed the serpent, men severed themselves from their own snake power. In the West, all snake-like body movements have come to be associated with the purportedly immoral and licentious nature of woman. Today, snake-like movements are still considered primarily feminine and, for a man, effeminate. This misunderstanding of snake energy is particularly evident in the history of belly dance, originally a Middle Eastern form of sacred movement meditation, but which has been degraded as a form of sexual entertainment. Though many renowned belly dancers of the past and present have in fact been men, Western culture discourages men from moving and thinking in nonlinear, serpentine ways.

The Evil Serpent

Many myths and fairy tales recount the defeat of a sly, malicious serpent. The serpent is a guardian of boundaries. In its negative form, the serpent represents that within us which rigidly defends these boundaries, obstructing change, and denying fluidity. The fire-breathing dragon jealously brooding over its treasures is the diseased ego that will not allow its boundaries to expand. In its positive, life-giving form, however, the serpent embodies the healing power of vibration and the rhythmic alternation of contraction and release. In this case, the serpent is the ally of what we previously described as the healthy ego.

The defeat of the evil serpent implies the victory of love and life's rhythms over the forces of fear and death. This is the inner meaning of the myth of Krishna—an incarnation of the Hindu god Vishnu—and Kaliya, a cruel and arrogant serpent-monster. Kaliya lived in the Jamuna river with his many beautiful serpent-wives and wrought terrible destruction among the villagers, with whom Krishna lived as a young boy. Kaliya brandished the fiery poison of his breath as his weapon; under Kaliya's breath everything alive shriveled and blackened. He poisoned the sacred River of Life in this manner, leaving no source of water for the villagers and animals to drink and bathe in. When Krishna heard of the villagers' distress, he jumped into the river and summoned the monster. While the terrified villagers watched, Krishna performed an exuberant dance of joy upon Kaliya's head, leaving the serpent defeated, bruised, and battered by the young god's feet. Yet instead of killing Kaliya, Krishna gave in to the pleas of the great snake and his wives, allowing them to depart humbled and willing forever afterward to leave the villagers in peace.

In this story, the serpent clearly represents a force that denies and endangers the rhythms of life. Similarly, the evil serpent within us is generated and nourished by what I call false fear. True fear serves the purpose of self-preservation by signaling the presence of a threat; false fear on the other hand is a human anomaly rooted in our extraordinary ability to fantasize. Not a day passes without our fantasizing the most atrocious scenes of violence, torture, and suffering of every imaginable kind. False fear causes us to harden our boundaries in defense, even at times when such hardening is inappropriate, and poisons the river of life with the venom of paranoid fear. A form of self-torture, false fear does not lead to appropriate self-protective action but causes paralysis and disease.

Enslaved by false fear, our protective boundaries become prison bars that hold us within the narrow confines of the known and prevent expansion into the unknown. Translated into the physiology of the human body, false fear manifests as unrelenting tension that causes our muscles to tighten and harden, never allowing them to relax. Since the body automatically responds to the mind's alarm signals—without distinguishing between fantasized and real danger—a body in the grip of false fear can never fully relax.

Kundalini

Indian mysticism teaches that our very life depends on the presence of the serpentine energy within our bodies called Kundalini, the Coiled One. One of the earliest surviving works of art from India (dated around 2000 B.C.E.) shows two meditators backed by two gigantic serpents with unfurled hoods. Among the various serpentine energies of the body, Kundalini is the prima donna—sensational, dramatic, and surrounded by an aura of mystique and danger. Kundalini is considered to be the microcosmic manifestation of the Goddess within the individual human body. Lying dormant at the base of the spine until awakened, she moves up the spine towards union with Shiva, the masculine aspect of consciousness seated in the crown of the head. Many Eastern teachers believe the awakening of Kundalini within the human body to be an essential prerequisite of enlightenment. Like the king cobra she is associated with, Kundalini is both magnificent and deadly, and must be treated with the utmost respect and caution. The Indian yogi Gopi Krishna has written a compelling account of his experience with the inadvertently awakened Kundalini, whose tremendous power, like a stray lightning bolt, nearly destroyed his life and burned his body to an ember.[8]

Obviously, a world of difference separates the experience of suddenly awakening Kundalini, who can terrify and blind the devotee with her power, from the experience of gently moving into harmony with the serpentine energies of your body. All wave movements of the body are manifestations of Kundalini. But the difference between them and the classic Kundalini experience is as great as the difference between the voltage of the electric current that illumines a light bulb and the gargantuan power of a lightning bolt. The arousal of the body's latent Kundalini is often accompanied by violent symptoms of pain, flashing light, sleeplessness, and so on. Unfortunately, in the West, many people undergoing a Kundalini experience are heavily sedated or even institutionalized since the mainstream medical profession has no understanding of these processes. Like lightning, Kundalini is no plaything but rather, in the words of Gopi Krishna, "the queen and architect of the living organism, having the power to mould it, transform it, or even to destroy it as she will."[9] Those paths of spiritual practice that aim at purposefully awakening the Kundalini are among the most dangerous and require the highest degree of skill, purity, and commitment of both teacher and student.

At the same time we should bear in mind that the body is an electromagnetic system, and Kundalini—as the force that governs its currents—is omnipresent. To speak of a "Kundalini experience" is in some ways misleading, since our entire life is a Kundalini experience. Kundalini expresses herself through sexuality; Kundalini is the force that causes visions and other psychic experiences, making the meditator's body tremble, go into trance, or dance in ways his conscious mind could never devise. Kundalini is also the source of the power that flows through a healer's hands. Kundalini, like electricity, becomes frightening only when it overpowers the body, and even then, if the process can be allowed to run its course, it will in most cases reveal itself as an initiation into higher levels of consciousness.

The Serpent and the Unconscious

When serpentine movements ripple involuntarily through skin and muscles, we become aware of impulses arising from deep within, over which we have little or no control. We should welcome such involuntary vibrations as symptoms of the subconscious orchestrating its own healing. They penetrate to the deepest layers of the body, rhythmically shaking loose what is rigid or petrified, what has been imprisoned and repressed, opening and balancing the energetic passageways of the body. Illness is a disturbance of body energy; certain forms of body-oriented therapies, such as bioenergetics, use special exercises to encourage involuntary rippling and trembling movements. The smaller and faster the vibrations, the deeper their power to penetrate, and the greater their healing potential. As Kaye Hoffman points out, one of the Latin names of god is *Tremendum,* literally, that which causes us to tremble.[10] This trembling should not be confused with fear. I have often experienced such trembling when opening my being fully to the presence of spirit. I imagine that as the higher energy enters our body, it realigns the very molecules and cells as it passes through.

The inability to allow involuntary body movements is usually associated with psychological rigidity and fear of letting go. Whether you respond with fear or with exhilaration as serpentine movements rise up from of the depths of the body depends upon your relationship to the subconscious. Any form of involuntary movement can be a frightening experience when the ego-structure is either very weak and in danger of disintegration, or, as is far more common, overly fearful and controlling. During movement meditation, you may experience your body taking over and moving independently of your conscious volition. Your hands may move into certain *mudras* (sacred gestures) quite unfamiliar to you. Sometimes people begin to shake, tremble, sing, or chant. In one of my classes, a woman found herself sitting in the classic Indian pose of the dark goddess, Kali, with her eyes rolled upward and her tongue sticking out. She had never heard of Kali, and so she was quite frightened by the experience. But such phenomena are no cause for fear. They subside on their own after a time, and the only possible danger involved stems from the attempts of well-meaning onlookers to forcefully and abruptly wrench the person out of her deep state, leading to a sense of incompleteness and disorientation.

It is also quite common for people to spontaneously visualize snakes in movement meditation or to subsequently dream of snakes. The appearance of dangerous and threatening snakes in one's dreams does not necessarily represent a fear of sexuality, as some people assume. The issues involved are more likely related to the ego's struggle to adjust to increasing levels of energy.

Making Peace with the Serpent

The suppression of our connection with serpentine energies has alienated modern men and women from nature and from our own bodies. It may well be that our alienation from nature was a necessary step in the individuation process of humankind, just as an adolescent may rebel against a powerful mother in order to find her own path. The greatest achievement of patriarchal civilization has been the remarkable technical and scientific knowledge it has amassed, an achievement most certainly motivated by the desire to know and control nature, rather than be controlled by it. But perhaps now our self-consciousness has matured sufficiently to allow a reconnection with the serpentine energies within and around us, without striving to dominate them. In this way, a healing may take place between humankind and nature, as well as between masculine and feminine principles, allowing the reemergence of what Riane Eisler calls a "partnership model."[11] Instead of slaying the serpent, we can approach it respectfully, as the Hopi Indians do, greeting it as the sacred messenger of the earth and befriending it once again.

CHAPTER SIX: MEDITATIONS

Befriending the Snake

RECOMMENDED MUSIC: Meditation or rhythmic music

This meditation invites you to drop out of your head into your body. Attuning ourselves to wave movements is not simply a question of moving more gracefully or fluidly. You are using your body as a radio, tuning in to a certain vibratory frequency that will affect not only your body, but your entire being.

This meditation can be adapted for people in wheelchairs or those with other disabilities. It can be practiced in any position—standing up, sitting, or even lying down. The meditation will benefit you even if you practice it for only five minutes, but you can also spend hours meditating on the subtle aspects of the serpent movements. Use snake movements regularly to loosen or heal a particular area in your body, especially to work with such spinal problems as scoliosis.

Plant your feet firmly on the earth. Close your eyes, and breathe. Throughout this meditation, keep your knees soft and flexible.

Gently sway back and forth. Feel your entire spinal column. Try to visualize it as a snake. Move your head around, and feel the smooth movement of a snake's head, the alertness of its senses. Imagine that your eyes are located on the sides of your head, near your temples.

Sway slowly, like a snake mesmerized by the melody of a flute. For now, let your arms simply hang by your sides, relaxed, only your spine moving, your neck, your head. Nothing else.

The serpent is a creature of the earth. As you breathe, be aware of your feet contacting the ground. Inhaling, invite the earth's energy to enter your spine at its very base. Let your tailbone feel its connection with the earth.

As you begin, your spine may feel like a cold snake, a snake with a still, stiff, slow body. With every breath you take, send a gentle wave of movement through it.

There is energy within your spine, and the more you focus on it, and breathe through it, the more it will expand. As it increases, it will want to move. It moves in its own way, guided by a wisdom inaccessible to your conscious mind. You need not control it, or make it move. Your task is merely to remember your breath, and to surrender.

Let the snake begin to show you where it wants to stretch, where it wants to contract. Every part of a snake moves, and every part of your own spine can move, from the tailbone to the base of your skull. Enjoy its sensuality, its sure knowledge of where pleasure is to be found.

Feel your entire spinal column, from the base all the way to the top of your head, as a single unit. Nothing moves independently in a snake. A wave of motion that begins at its tail flows through all the way to its head.

Let the snake begin to dance with the energy you are sending through it. Call upon it, invite it, talk to it, sing to it. Ask it to awaken in you, to dance through you. Let your spine become warm and fluid like a snake that has been lying on hot rocks, on the sun-drenched earth.

And once your spine is warm, begin to include your entire body in the dance. See if the waves you have generated in your spine want to radiate out through the rest of your body.

Waves might start at the top of your head and flow through to your tailbone, or they may flow from the tailbone upward. They may start in your heart and flow out your fingertips.

Keep your knees soft, and keep breathing. Move with the gentleness of water.

Look deeply within your body and sense the energy enveloping your spinal column and flowing through the spine itself—a streaming through your very center. Sometimes that streaming needs to free itself through shivering, shaking, trembling. A sloughing off of old tensions and fear. Give in to that trembling should it arise. Surrender to it, breathing deeply, just moving through it. Offer no resistance.

Let go of any attempt to control or understand what your body is doing. The serpent has its own wisdom, of which your conscious mind knows nothing.

All around you, energy is flowing, vibrating, pulsating, and all these pulsations are affecting your body. Let the dance unfold, trusting in its perfection. The dance of the serpent is a dance of healing, of moving into at-oneness with all that is.

Dance as long as you want. When you begin to tire and want to slow down, lie down on the earth or settle into your seat.

Your large movements have awakened the serpentine energy in you and have generated healing heat. So keep moving, but allow the ripples and undulations to become very slight, very subtle. You can keep moving throughout your entire spine, or you can focus in on one area that is asking for special attention.

If an area feels stiff or painful, move around it, surrounding it with movement and vibration, carefully exploring the edges. Approach your body with gentleness and with compassionate acceptance. Find ways of moving that feel pleasurable and healing.

Use your breath and your focused awareness to send tiny waves and ripplets into painful or numb areas, bringing healing and life-force into them. On the inhalations, send in light and vibration. On the exhalations, let go. Even the tightest knot is not really solid or impenetrable. Imagine that tiny pulsations and undulations of powerful healing light are entering the area.

You are now beginning to explore vibrations that are so subtle they straddle the borderline between the mental and the physical.

At this level, it is impossible to distinguish between actual physical movements and imaginary, intended ones. Understand that your intention is entirely real and can produce physical results.

The subtler the pulsation you work with, the more mental concentration you need. If your mind strays, gently bring it back. It is not used to focusing on something so subtle and intangible. But what is happening here is not imaginary. It is very real.

Watch these subtle snake movements arise and disappear spontaneously. Just observe without interfering, as if you were watching a snake in the wild. Stay present, and maintain awareness of your breath. Open yourself to a sense of reverence as you invite the life-force to move through you on its mysterious paths.

The movements become smaller, until only tiny ripplets of energy are flowing through your spine.

Finally, there is almost no movement at all visible from without. And yet, you can still feel the snake movements pulsating through your spine. Even when your body becomes quite still, you can feel the serpent's presence within your spine. Sense everything in your body and all around you pulsating with its own rhythm, dancing its own snake dance.

Rest in stillness as long as you desire.

Breath Waves

RECOMMENDED MUSIC: Silence or meditation music

Symbolically the snake belongs to both the unconscious underworld and to the highest realms of consciousness. In the act of breathing, these two worlds meet. For breathing can be either conscious or unconscious, voluntary or involuntary. Working with breath, one can draw the turmoil of deeply buried memories to the surface, but one can also move into states of blissful peace.

Breathing is not a linear function consisting of two parts, inhalation and exhalation. Breath, like water, moves in waves. In this meditation, don't think of your breath as moving in and out, or up and down, in a linear fashion. Regarding breath as a wave will add a new dimension to your experience of it. While the rational mind is dualistic and linear, and tends to think in terms of "either/or"—inhalation or exhalation—the truth of the body is serpentine and multidimensional.

Consider the Chinese yin-yang symbol. Its dark and light segments form a wave pattern. Where the light side is fullest, it is pregnant with the seed of darkness; where the dark area is fullest, it contains the seed of light. All wave movements, including your breath, follow this pattern. When you inhale, the air you breathe in contains the seed of your exhalation. As this seed grows and your lungs expand, your inhalation slows down until it gently fades into the exhalation. Breathing out, you can feel the seed of the next inhalation. By using your breath in this way, your breathing becomes an ever-present link between the mind and all the other wave motions of your body.

Consider the breath as moving through four phases. Sit down comfortably, and start to breathe according to the following pattern:

1. Inhale.
2. Hold your breath for two seconds.
3. Exhale.
4. Hold your breath for two seconds.

The holding should be brief enough to be effortless. When you try to hold your breath for a long time, you will find that you automatically block your throat to prevent exhaling. Try to avoid doing this—keep the breath's passageway clear. Just pause briefly after inhaling and after exhaling.

Now, add the visualization of the serpent-wave. As you pause, imagine the downward wave turning upward, and the upward turning down. In the silence, visualize the movement continuing and turning.

When you stop inhaling, you can imagine the breath soaring upward like a ball thrown toward the sky, then slowing down until it seems to hang suspended in the air for a brief moment.

Then it begins to fall, first slowly, then gathering speed. And finally,

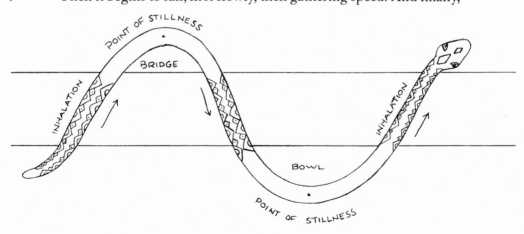

the breath-ball enters your body again and you exhale, moving down, down, down.

Again the same process: you exhale and pause, and in the stillness, the movement continues downward, slows to a brief instance of perfect stillness, and then reverses into the upward movement. And as the upward movement enters you, it becomes a new inhalation.

Once you have discovered the wave, you will no longer need to pause between breaths. Just breathe easily. Stay present, watch your breath and ride the waves.

Breath Waves (Variation)

Begin watching your breath waves as described above.

Now, as your inhalation turns into the exhalation, visualize the movement as an arching bridge.

And as your exhalation turns into the inhalation, visualize a bowl.

Continue to watch your breath in this way until you clearly see or feel the two arches: the bridge arch and the bowl arch.

And in your breath, they are not separate, but one.

The arches are like containers, like cupped hands. The bridge is arched in such a way that it can receive and contain the earth's radiance. The bowl is shaped in such a way that it can receive and contain the sky's energy.

Now practice seeing the bridge and the bowl, until you can not only feel them clearly in your breath pattern, but can feel the exact moment of stillness: the moment of silence after the inhalation, which is the highest point of the bridge. And the moment of silence after the exhalation, which is the lowest point of the bowl.

In this moment, stillness of the body meets silence of the mind. This is the moment of utter silence, of magic, of suspension between two breaths as well as between two worlds, the world of time and the timeless. Feel, now, the intersection of time and infinity.

So as you inhale and pause, awaken to that flash of presence: you are in the very center of the bridge, an open hand cupped over the world, meeting the earth in a moment of timeless communication.

And as you exhale and pause, again be aware: feel yourself to be as the open bowl of a plowed field waiting for the rain, the sunshine, the touch of the sky.

Continue for at least ten minutes.

CHAPTER SEVEN

Rhythm and Trance

This core of drumming is as the organic axis of the spiritual cosmos, around which all the temporal elements of ritual are centered. It is upon these pulsations that, for the most part, the loa [gods] are brought forward; and, as they can be led in on water, or on rum, or on the fire of burning rum, so, innerly, it is as if they were brought in on the stream of blood, pulsed not by the individual personal heart, but by some older, deeper, cosmic heart—the drums.

MAYA DEREN

Taken by the sound of the music, the dancer enters into another level of reality, both communal and universal. In these circle dances, done in community celebrations, each individual has his or her rightful place. Not only the beautiful, the elegant, or sophisticated belong, but everyone. The dance possesses an invisible force that can draw a person farther than he or she imagines. When one is truly taken by the music, one becomes capable of movements that one could not have willingly done otherwise. Some people become so possessed by the dance that for several days afterwards they no longer have the same sense of reality as the average person.

YAYA DIALLO

The Rhythmic Universe

HINDUISM HAS GIVEN us the magnificent image of Shiva Nataraj, lord of the cosmic dance. From his stamping feet the rhythms of creation burst forth: the rhythms of breath and heartbeat, the rotations of gigantic galaxies and planets with their suns and moons, and the immeasurably rapid vibrations that constitute what we perceive as solid matter. The precise patterns of Shiva's intricate choreography translate into musical harmonies, the changing of the seasons, and the structure of snowflakes, sunflowers, and crystals. As Shiva Nataraj dances, his uplifted arm shakes the *damaru,* a small hourglass-shaped drum made by joining the skulls of a man and a woman at the crown, and covering them with skin to form a two-sided instrument. Thus, even Shiva's drum itself speaks of the rhythmic interplay of male and female, death and life.

Nearly every traditional culture regards sound as sacred, the audible manifestation of a primal rhythmic force that harmonizes the universe. According to Hindu tradition, rhythmic vibration is no mere element of creation; rather, creation *is* rhythm. Each one of us is a special manifestation of rhythmic patterning, embodying both collective and uniquely personal

Shiva Nataraja, lord of the cosmic dance.
India, 11th century.

rhythms. Like a tree or flower, a human being shares a common archetypal pattern with every other member of the species, yet each manifests the common pattern in his own way. The medieval mystic Meister Eckhart once remarked that just as a seed can only grow into the particular tree it is meant to be, so human beings are god-seeds and can only become the unique manifestation of god that each is destined to embody. We consist of vibration, and each of us shall only fulfill our potential by embodying the unique vibrational or rhythmic pattern that is our own.

Observing the Rhythms of Nature

In prehistoric times, understanding nature's rhythmic patterns was a question of survival for humankind. If the rhythms of an animal could be embodied through dance and drumming, then that animal could be hunted and killed. The first step in gaining control over natural phenomena was to observe their patterns. The design of a pomegranate, a beehive, a fingerprint, or a molecule expresses its essence. To understand the design is to draw near to the creator's mind. The earliest art forms were attempts to grasp and reproduce natural patterns and designs: to paint the body of the deer, to drum the rhythm of rain and thunderstorm, to dance the movements of the snake and jaguar. Through their art, human beings encoded and handed down knowledge of nature's laws from one generation to the next.

Sacred art reflects and celebrates the rhythms of creation. The ancient Greeks believed that cosmic music accompanied the heavenly spheres in their revolving dances and that all melodic harmony derived from it. Art forms, such as Indian music and dance, Muslim calligraphy, decorative arts and architecture, and medieval European brocades, all consist of intricate patterns woven from colors, numbers, and movement. Each design reflects cosmic order in its precision, beauty, and infinite creativity. A Gothic cathedral expresses the accumulated experience of many generations in the procession of soaring arches, and the geometry of its faceted windows. In many cultures, drumming conveys the rhythms of seasons, tides, and moon cycles, as well as those of the individual human life. Rhythm is the reflection of harmony in the universe; through music and dance, we achieve harmony with the cosmos.

Rhythm and Sacred Geometry

Our sense of hearing is only one of the many ways we respond to rhythm. Our eyes take in visual patterning, our intellect perceives mathematical logic, and our entire body senses patterns of touch and movement. These sensory inroads are what psychiatrist and author Arnold Mindell calls "channels."[1] All such channels are sensitive to rhythm, and they are all interconnected: rhythmic information received through one channel may be translated into a different one. An example of this is the work of the contemporary German musician Peter Hamel, who translated planetary movements into sound, making audible the legendary music of the spheres. Other evidence of this phenomenon is the ability of deaf people to perceive musical rhythm proprioceptively through the skin, as babies do in the womb.

In dance, patterns of movement, abstract geometric patterns, and musical rhythms combine into a single experience; the rhythms of the drum convert into images and body movements, arches and turns, spirals and waves. Time patterns can be represented through patterns in space—a three-beat rhythm can be expressed as a triangle, a four-beat rhythm as a square. Conversely the circle, a spatial symbol of wholeness, corresponds to a single, continuous sound vibration. Tibetan chanting quiets the meditator's mind by using unbroken circle of the AUM mantra to achieve a state of oneness with the universe. The tranquilizing effect of the sound vibration can be further heightened by simultaneously meditating on the visual image of a circle.

Along similar lines, many traditions teach that certain geometric designs and rhythms contain the living presence of nature spirits, gods and goddesses, and these forms and rhythms can be used to communicate with the spiritual realm. "Your body is sacred vibration," says an ancient Sanskrit hymn to the Goddess. In Hinduism, the vibrational pattern of a deity is believed to be contained within either a sound vibration *(mantra)*, a visual image or geometric design *(yantra)*, or a sacred gesture *(mudra)*; all of these may be used in conjunction with one another. In Haiti, each deity is represented by a design or *vevier,* as well as through certain rhythms that are drummed to summon the presence of that deity. Many traditional African religions call in the deities by drumming their particular rhythmic patterns.

The Intersection of Time and Eternity

One of the unique experiments linking human consciousness and the realm of archetypal patterning took place in the Findhorn community in northern Scotland. Findhorn, originally located on barren sandy soil, is today the center of large flourishing gardens and farms tended by a spiritual community of several hundred people. It was founded in the nineteen sixties by just three dedicated people, among them a Canadian woman, Dorothy Maclean. Dorothy Maclean had the ability to communicate with the *Devas,* or nature spirits. Sending messages and information through her, the Devas guided the cultivation of the miraculously successful Findhorn gardens. Without the cooperation of these nature forces, Findhorn's gardens would have been incapable of bringing forth fruits and vegetables anywhere near the size and quality of those harvested by the Findhorn community. The gardeners listened to and followed the archetypal rhythms of creation the Devas revealed, such as the voice of the apple tree:

> Whatever happens, we hold the archetypal pattern immovable. If alteration is necessary, we hold the alteration as part of the pattern. Then it is unchanging, a great steadiness stemming from the eternal peace of God. The incredible activity of our kingdom clusters around the patterns, making sure that they are brought into form perfectly, serving them endlessly. We state this because we would have you realize that you too have the same quality of undeviating devotion to a pattern, which you can hold in rock-like peace under God.[2]

Rhythm lives at the crossroads of the abstract realm of order and the embodied realm of creative flux; the experiencing of rhythm allows us to align these two realms within ourselves. Meditating on the symmetry and precision of archetypal patterns fine tunes our being and helps us slough off vibrational disturbances accumulated through daily living. As poet Rainer Maria Rilke said, "Do not be bewildered by the surfaces; in the depths all becomes law."[3] Geometric forms, gods and goddesses, musical rhythms, and movement patterns all point toward what the Hindus call *dharma,* Christians, Jews, and Muslims call the will of God, what in China is called the *Tao.* Meditation on these expressions of the archetypal realm brings peace and centeredness, as life's patterns rearrange themselves and fall into their rightful places.

Abstract Pattern and Physical Embodiment

Like rhythmic patterns, geometric forms belong to the realm of abstractions. Natural plant, animal, and mineral forms are based upon these blueprints. But in its physical manifestation, no form is mathematically precise. No natural rhythm or pattern is perfectly consistent. Similarly, when you practice a movement meditation based on a perfect geometric form such as the circle, spiral, or figure eight, your actual body movements will only approximate the geometric figure. Every rose embodies the same perfect pattern, yet no two are precisely identical; each one manifests the blueprint in its own unique way.

Individuation from the pattern should not be regarded as an imperfection or flaw. Every face and every body is slightly asymmetrical and, far from spoiling an individual's beauty, this asymmetry actually enhances it. Asymmetry simply reveals how, within the body, universal design intersects with individual development, the eternal overlapping the temporal. The same principle applies when you visualize a circle or a triangle while you dance—you are actually meditating on the relationship between the mental image and the physical sensations of your body's response to that image, thus harmonizing a universal pattern and your individual embodiment of that pattern.

Rhythmic Healing

Patterns and rhythms are expressions of cosmic order; by understanding them, we understand nature's deeper forces. But we can also reverse this process and, through the use of rhythm, introduce harmony and order where there is disturbance and chaos.

Traditional societies assumed that, just as the rhythms and patterns of nature greatly affect human beings, musical and rhythmic vibrations also influence natural events in beneficial or harmful ways. All over the globe, very specific forms of music, dance, and rhythm have evolved to accompany the important events of human experience: birth, death, the sowing of seeds, harvesting, puberty initiations, marriage, and so on. In many societies, rhythm is believed to affect the weather, the growth of plants, the behavior of animals, and the relationship between the human and the spirit world. The healer-drummer Yaya Diallo, from the Minianka tribe in Mali, says that after a crime or disaster has occurred there, it is essential to heal the disturbed spirits of the land by playing the specific rhythms that calm them and restore peace. He deplores the neglect of such healing rituals throughout the North American continent where he now lives.[4]

From the familiar, rhythmic patterns of our physical existence—such as the rhythmic alternations of the changing seasons—we derive much of our sense of being at home in a nurturing universe. Indeed our very sanity depends on being grounded in these rhythms. To lose our sense of rhythm is as terrifying, fragmenting, and disorienting an experience as losing the ground under our feet in an earthquake. Rhythm reminds us of what the Tibetan teacher Chögyam Trungpa calls "the basic goodness of the universe"[5]; rhythm assures us that some fundamentally reliable power operates throughout nature. Both physical and mental disease are forms of rhythmic disturbance, and require, as Yaya Diallo points out, the assistance of those who possess the knowledge of rhythmic healing:

> In the Minianka villages of Fienso and Zangasso, the musicians were
> healers, the healers musicians. The word musician itself implies the

role of healer. From the Minianka perspective, it is inconceivable that the responsibilities for making music and restoring health should be separate, as they are in the West.[6]

Among the Minianka, health is considered a state of harmony with the rhythms of society and nature, an alignment with the basic order of life. Conversely, disease is regarded as a state of rhythmic disharmony. Many mentally disturbed people have little or no sense of rhythm, having literally lost touch with the ground of their existence. Unfortunately, Western culture has no understanding of the healing potential of rhythm—and the societies that have developed such wisdom, such as the Minianka, are rapidly losing their priceless and ancient knowledge to the process of modernization.

Like many African spiritual cultures, Korean shamanism also possesses a highly sophisticated art of rhythmic healing. Reinhard Flatischler, an Austrian percussion and rhythm teacher, underwent such a healing while studying in Korea with a man who was both a master drummer and a shaman. After some months in that country, Reinhard fell seriously ill. Conventional medicines failed to improve his condition, a form of dysentery, and although he wanted to fly home, he rapidly became too weak to do so. His teacher, upon returning from a trip and finding Reinhard in this condition, told him that a healing ceremony would be conducted. Reinhard was reluctant:

> I was stunned. I felt debilitated, and my limbs were in pain. How would I be able to tolerate the sheer volume of this music, which I had experienced so many times, in this condition? How could Korean rhythms possibly improve my condition when the strongest medicines had failed to help me? Suddenly, I felt that these shamanic ceremonies were no more than dark superstition, and I was aware of having lost my faith in the effect of the rhythms in my state of illness. I was very afraid.
>
> The next day, when Kim Suk Jul arrived with a few friends to pick me up, I was determined that I was not going to allow this ceremony to be imposed upon me. Although I was not immediately able to ex-

press my resistance, he seemed to sense it. He stood next to me for a long time without saying a word. Something emanated from him that allowed me to feel the depth of my trust in him.

But by the time we reached the place of the ceremony, I was terrified again. Kim Suk Jul had disappeared, and I felt alone, lost in a world of dark powers. The pain increased, and I felt trapped in a terrible nightmare.

With a roar the music began and the harsh sound of the instruments ripped my thoughts apart. I fell into a state in which thinking was impossible. Although I still perceived my surroundings, I was suspended in an entirely different world. It was a world of feelings which I had never experienced before. I felt parts of my body shift, fall apart, and come back together again. I saw my body assume various colors, and each of these colors triggered a certain, indescribable bodily sensation within me. More and more I fell into a state of which I have no recollection.

When I regained consciousness, the sun was shining into the little room in Kim Suk Jul's house, where I was lying. I was very tired, but I could feel that I was better. Soon I fell into a long, deep sleep.[7]

Entering Trance

The shamanic drum is not primarily a musical instrument, but a vehicle that transports one into other dimensions of reality. Beaten in a simple, monotonous rhythm, it produces an undulating wave of sound and silence, rich in overtones. This drumbeat becomes the primordial serpent-wave that the shaman rides into nonmaterial realms of existence, returning with healing knowledge. The simple beat of a drum is one of the most powerful consciousness-altering tools human beings possess. It hypnotizes the rational, analytical side of the mind, which guards the entrance to other dimensions and that—like Cerberus, the mythological Greek watchdog of the underworld—must drift to sleep before we can cross into the threshold of the beyond.

Trance states often occur when our limits of physical endurance are surpassed. For example, on one occasion I had to give a solo dance performance although I was quite ill. As I began, the music gradually quickened into a firework of rhythms, five beats layered upon three upon seven upon four. For the first half hour I cursed and sweated. But then, instead of collapsing as I had feared I would, my body took over and my thoughts dropped away. From one moment to the next, my sick, struggling, angry self dissolved, and with it, my exhaustion. The music and I became one, and the rhythms simply flowed through me while I watched, enthralled. Each movement was crystal clear. The music seemed to have slowed down, and time spread open like a fan, allowing me to savor every gesture, every circling of the arm, every sideways glance. The fever disappeared after the performance and within a day I recovered completely.

During this trance the healing rhythms connected me to a reservoir of infinite energy. The ego cannot be forced to surrender, but certain circumstances—and dancing beyond the limits of physical endurance is one of them—foster altered states of consciousness. In tribal cultures, sacred ceremonies include trance dances, during which the participants cross over the boundary and enter nonordinary realms. In this state, they may pierce their flesh with hooks, take burning coals into their mouths, or behave in other ways that seem to require superhuman endurance or miraculous powers. In such a society, everyone will at some point have had the experience of transcending the ego. There is a strong communal basis of trust in the trance experience, knowledge of the symptoms one may experience in the process, and understanding of its value for the individual and the community.

Our own culture has eliminated all such rituals from social life, replacing the individual's own spiritual experience with the power of priesthood. The priest's authority separates the congregation from direct communion with the higher powers. It is significant that along with banning rhythmic trance, we have also forbidden the use of mind-altering drugs. Shamanic cultures use these substances in the same way they use drumming, namely as a vehicle for passage into the nonordinary realms of being. Tribal societies hold both rhythm and mind-altering plants sacred, and indeed both are often used in conjunction with one another.

Many religions worldwide include the use of drugs in their sacrament, while others consider sobriety the greatest virtue. By using a drug, we are taking the outside material world into ourselves, not only into our bodies—a notion acceptable to Western medicine—but into our minds and consciousness. If such an act is to serve effectively as a sacrament, we must believe that divine spirit inhabits the drug itself. In other words, there must be a deep trust in the essential god-nature of the physical world. If we believe human beings possess spirit but that a mushroom or cactus does not, we cannot appreciate the plant as a kind of teacher. Only if we accept that it embodies spirit may we learn from the plant what its essence may reveal.

More than any previous one, Western industrial society is plagued by drug and alcohol addiction. The source of the attraction to drugs lies in a basic human craving for mystical experience; addiction follows in the wake of unsatisfied spiritual hunger. We all share, to a degree, the need to experience nonordinary states of consciousness. Unless society respects this need and provides safe and communally sanctioned rites of passage, people are bound to pursue any substance that promises to induce an altered state. The need for ecstasy is basic to human nature and cannot be suppressed indefinitely. "Sex, drugs, and rock 'n' roll" are, in essence, no new phenomena; they represent a modern equivalent to ancient keys to the transcendent.

Everything sacred holds great power, yet all power can be misused: the problem lies not in the tool itself, but in the spiritual ignorance of our society. The policy of surrounding the trance state with an aura of fear and illegality stems from such ignorance, and its result is tragic stories of souls lost for lack of guidance.

The Heartbeat

As we are embraced within the infinite, infinity builds its nest within us. One breaks into two, and the two know, in their embrace, that they are one. The wave, the snake, the yin-yang symbol, and the divine lovers are symbols of the interplay of oneness and duality. Their acoustic equivalent is the heartbeat: the rhythmic alternation of sound and silence.

Human beings respond to the heartbeat in an instinctual and primal way, not only through our sense of hearing, but with our entire body. In the womb, the embryo meditates on the mother's heartbeat for nine months. Even before its sense of hearing develops, it feels the heartbeat through its skin. This is our first experience with rhythm—perhaps our first sensory experience of any kind. After birth, each time a baby nurses, it returns not only to the safety of the mother's body, but to the steady reassurance of her heartbeat. As adults, our need for connection with the heartbeat does not diminish. Its source merely shifts from the human mother to the universal mother whose heartbeat speaks to us through the rhythms of nature, of art, poetry, music, and dance.

The heartbeat provides the basis for all other manifestations of rhythm. We may learn to drum, speak, dance, or clap any number of very complex rhythms, but unless the knowledge of the basic heartbeat is securely anchored in your body, any new knowledge is built on sand. All these complex rhythmic patterns will collapse and disintegrate as soon as a conflicting rhythm challenges them. Only when you are sure of the basic beat—when you know it in your bones—can you hold your own rhythm with clarity and assurance.

In the early twentieth century, when African music first gained popularity in Western societies, critics considered it "primitive." Rhythm is indeed primitive—in the sense that it allows us to experience our own primordial nature. If today rhythm has once again entered the foreground of the Western music scene, we can point to the enormous influence of contemporary African and Eastern music. Yet at a deeper level, the driving beat of modern popular music is a symptom of Western civilization's longing to find its way back to the heartbeat of the universe. Westerners are becoming increasingly conscious of a deep yearning for harmonious communication with the cosmos that emerges so naturally during the rhythmic ecstasy of tribal dancing and drumming.

Rhythm as the Basis of Community

Rhythm is, above all, an expression of *relationship*. Through rhythm, people describe their relationship with nature, and with each other. The most sophisticated rhythmic art forms have invariably evolved in societies that maintained their connection to nature. Each had a strong communal tradition founded upon a bedrock of firm social and spiritual values. By contrast, since the industrial revolution, Western culture has been obsessed with the dream of conquering nature, and with the ideas of personal freedom and individualism. As a result, rhythm is the least-developed aspect of Western music. With the loss of "the pattern that connects,"[8] the basis for communal play has been gradually eroded. Compared to the complexity of Indian or African music, classical Western music is rhythmically underdeveloped, confining itself for the most part to three or four beat rhythms.

Rhythm is medicine for both the individual and the community, and communal drumming and dancing unite celebration and healing. In traditional cultures, people gather regularly for festivals and rituals; drumming and dancing may continue for days on end. Completely immersing themselves in rhythm, the people become attuned to nature's rhythms and to the rhythms of their tribe. Like the flow of blood to and from the heart, the dancers are drawn to the beat of the drums, leaving renewed, every cell in their bodies aligned with the common beat.

In modern life, we are accustomed to the experience of disharmony between our individual rhythms and those of society, yet such blatant disharmony is undoubtedly a state of disease. Modern life is extremely rhythmic, but its rhythms are based on the needs of industrial society; these mechanical rhythms have no connection whatsoever to the organic rhythms of nature.

Living in India, I saw how industrialists struggled to replace natural rhythms with mechanical ones in order to heighten production. Their employees were still accustomed to observing the natural cycles of their physical and spiritual life; despite their impoverished circumstances, they would stay away from work because of an important family celebration, a religious festival, or simply because they needed rest. Though many attribute such work habits to laziness and unreliability, these workers were far from lazy. Their social priorities simply stood at odds with those of a modern industrial society.

In a healthy society, rhythms and patterns of the individual, of the community, and of the cosmos complement each other, just as in a healthy body, cells and organs differ in their functions yet cooperate harmoniously.

Drummer Yaya Diallo reports that in his village, the musician-healers diagnose mental imbalance by watching the people dance. One sign of illness is movements that do not correspond to the particular individual's role in the community:

> While playing for community dancing, the Minianka musicians may sense disturbances as they manifest in people's dancing. When they amuse themselves, people reveal their serious side. As they relax, they let out their suppressed tendencies. The fact that each profession has its characteristic dance steps and movements gives valuable diagnostic indications of a person's inner balance. When a blacksmith comes to the center of the circle, the musicians play the smith's rhythm. If he dances like a fisherman, the musicians know right away that something is unbalanced with him.[9]

Among the Minianka, health is restored by leading the individual back into a state of alignment with the rhythms appropriate to his professional role in life and to his personal identity. These healers make use of what physics calls the principle of resonance or *entrainment*. Entrainment causes two similar, but slightly different rhythms to gradually fall into unison if they are placed in close proximity. A disturbed person's rhythmic patterns will shift according to the rhythms of the drums. In their use of rhythm as a tool for social integration, harmony, and cohesiveness, tribal societies show an intuitive understanding of entrainment.

In movement meditation circles, we frequently work with very simple movements for a long time. Linked by the heartbeat of the drums, we move in a circle. At first, most people are in their heads, trying hard to "get it right." I encourage people to look at each other, to breathe, to forget about their feet and feel their hearts and bellies instead. Rhythm is contagious— we catch it from one another. I have never met a person who, given enough time, would not eventually slip into rhythmic movement. This point almost always coincides with a moment of mindlessness, after the rhythmic drumming and the repetitiveness of movement has lulled the rational mind to sleep. After passing through excitement, resistance, exhaustion, and boredom, the mind eventually surrenders, finding little for it to grasp hold of amidst the utter simplicity of the movement, and one enters a light trance. Once entranced, the body will find its own way into the easiest, most natural and pleasurable form of movement, which is inevitably a wave-motion. In harmony with the wave, we are one with the basic rhythmic pulsations that structure both our lives and our bodies.

After some time, there may still be a few people who haven't caught on yet, and that too is fine. The more the circle relaxes into the rhythm, the more able it is to carry along those who need more time or are having difficulty. When one is learning something new, there must be space to make mistakes, to find the movement, lose it, and find it again. In group work, the experience of working with those who are out of step, or out of rhythm, is very important. Their difference may be a significant expression of something the group needs to pay attention to.

A movement meditation circle is in many ways a reflection of human society as a whole. It is not a place where spirituality is practiced in a secluded, shielded environment. All the issues that concern our daily life become part of our meditation. No community is healthy unless it can carry those members who are unable to carry their own weight, for whatever reason. Similarly, the power of the circle is all the more evident when it can continue to hold a common rhythm even when some of its members are out of sync. Circle members have described the healing that occurs by immersing themselves in rhythm as a sense of peace, of full-bodied presence, and of connection to the circle and to the earth.

The Function of Rock Music

With our loss of festivals and other social rituals dedicated to establishing our common rhythms, we have sacrificed a language that could unite us. In Western society, one of the very few places where one can experience a communal heartbeat rhythm is in a dance club. I have no doubt that many young people who frequent clubs go primarily in search of altered states of consciousness. In most clubs, however, the mind is not so much hypnotized as brutally beaten unconscious, then abandoned in a limbo of ghostlike figures, flashing lights, and general anonymity.

Rock music certainly resembles tribal drumming in that it allows people to go into a trance state, but the living sound of musicians has an entirely different effect on the human organism than electrically amplified sound does. Moreover, to the shaman, the trance is only the medium. The goal is balance and the attainment of healing wisdom. The commercial rock scene lacks, for the most part, both the intention to heal and the practical knowledge of healing that the shamanic cultures have developed to such a high degree. Fortunately, some Western musicians, such as Mickey Hart and Bobby McFerrin, are now beginning to create music that combines spiritual integrity and strong rhythm.

Indian art envisions Shiva's dance of creation as beginning with a steady stamping rhythm of his right foot: his dancing foot becomes the heartbeat of the cosmos. This basic beat represents the fundamental pattern that connects us. The most obvious development within the Western music scene for the last thirty years has been the intensity of the need for rhythmic immersion. In rock, reggae, and rap music, with the beat growing ever more basic, ever more insistent, we see the clear expression of our society's urgent need for rhythmic attunement. Indeed, we are starved for connection to the heartbeat, and we are starved for the spiritual dimensions of life. Whether one enjoys rock music or not is irrelevant. We must understand that it expresses a real and valid need of the social organism that longs to heal its alienation. Western society needs to go back to basics. Our popular music is telling us loud and clear that we need to find the heartbeat of our society, and we need to move beyond the fragmentation and alienation to affirm our connectedness.

CHAPTER SEVEN: MEDITATIONS

Tibetan Bowl Meditation

RECOMMENDED MUSIC: Your own voice

The Tibetan bowl is a round, metal bowl played by running a soft stick around its edge, until the bowl begins to "sing" with a resonant, mystical sound. As you move and chant, you will become this bowl, the vibrating, ringing center of the universe. The meditation is practiced in a sitting position and is therefore appropriate for many people who use a wheelchair.

Take a few minutes to stretch out and to loosen up. Then sit down comfortably with your spine upright, in such a way that it has space to move in all directions.

Close your eyes and call before your eyes the image of the circle. This circle is who you truly are: whole, perfect, and complete.

Feel the vertical heaven-earth axis as it runs through your spine, and notice where your tailbone connects with the earth.

Now invite a circular counterclockwise motion to arise and gently move you, but allow the circling to be so slight, so subtle, that you are unsure whether you are really moving or just imagining it. Then, very slowly, let it unfold.

As your body circles gently, let your inner vision dwell on the image of the circle. Everyone's circle is different. Some include colors and patterns. Some people see the circle as our planet, as the sun, as a flower, or an atom. If you are not a visually oriented person, simply imagine the circle. It is not important whether you can visualize it clearly or not.

The movement, too, will shift. At times, your entire spine will circle. Sometimes, only your pelvis will move, or only your heart area, or your head.

And from the center, something begins to radiate. Perhaps it is a sound, perhaps a light—they are one and the same. Listen carefully. Can you imagine a sound? Now, very softly, begin to hum it: Hmmmmmm. . . .

Feel the entire space within your circle resonating. Let go of controlling the vibration, of making it happen. Just let your voice pick up and amplify what is always there anyway: the hum of your blood, the vibration of your being.

From your circle, your sound-light radiates into the world. Its vibration carries with it the essence of who you are, your inner light. You become a star, a lighthouse, circling and humming your sound-light out into the universe.

Pattern Play

RECOMMENDED MUSIC: Either your own drumming or rhythmic music

True rhythm has both a fixed pattern and an inherent tendency toward change, without which evolution would be impossible. While mechanical rhythms remain (relatively) stable and are therefore essential to industrial production, everything in nature is rhythmic, but no rhythm remains unchanged forever. Your breath, your heartbeat, and even the rhythm of the earth's rotations around the sun fluctuate. The following meditation is for individual practice, but it also lends itself very well to group practice. In a group, form a circle so everyone can see everyone else. Agree on the initial movement pattern, and take off from there. This is good training in remaining fully present and aware, not only of yourself but of the whole group process. If you become distracted, you will miss changes in the group pattern. If you get caught in your private thoughts and ego, you may try to initiate changes willfully, instead of allowing them to arise naturally. Invariably, this will reflect back to you as a more or less blatant disharmony in the circle. When changes occur organically, however, no one person seems to be in charge; they simply arrive like ripe apples dropping into the grass. You can dance this meditation, or alternatively, you can drum it.

Begin by dancing or drumming freely for a few minutes.

Now find a simple pattern of rhythmic movement that pleases you, and keep repeating it. Repeat it as long as it feels right.

Listen carefully to the pattern. Be fully present with it. Notice whether it wants to remain the same, or whether it wants to change.

Try to let go of your mind. Release all attachment to whether the pattern should change or should remain the same.

When a change occurs, it will seem to arise of its own. You are not willfully initiating it, or consciously searching for a new movement. You simply notice that your body wants to move in a new way, or that the rhythm wants to shift.

Keep patiently repeating the pattern that is present. Let there be no attempt on your part to create anything whatsoever.

And be receptive. Listen carefully, so that when the change asks to happen, you are conscious enough to not miss it.

Never allow your movement to become mechanical. If you are moving mechanically, you have fallen asleep. Even if you repeat the same movement for an hour, don't fall into a rut. Stay awake and aware as you move.

Let your dance be alive with its own rhythm and energy. When that energy is ready, it will transform. If you can remain open to the transformation, there will be no end to the patterns and rhythms that arise.

Without forcing them, watch the rhythms arise and transform. Let go of wanting to entertain yourself or impress others by initiating change. Instead, let the changes come from within.

No attachment to the old way. No attachment to change, either. No impatience.

Allow each movement to find its resolution in the next. Watch the resolution arising spontaneously, effortlessly.

Thus, in your life, too, each situation contains within it its own resolution. Each pattern will give birth to the next, and the less you interfere with the natural rhythm of the process, the greater chance there is of harmony and ease.

Continue as long as you like, but allow yourself at least fifteen minutes. Then sit or lie down quietly for a few minutes.

The Seven Rainbow Rhythms

RECOMMENDED MUSIC: Your own voice, clapping, and stamping

The science of rhythm is closely related to numerology, astrology, and mathematics. In India, the most important rhythmic cycles are considered those of one, two, three, four, five, seven, and nine beats. Each of these rhythms has its own power, its own quality and mood, its own relationship to the other rhythms, and its own movements. Just as out of the fracturing of white light the seven colors of the rainbow emerge, so the seven rhythms of Eastern mythology are contained within the heartbeat of the universe and can be compared to the seven days of creation in biblical Genesis.

If you do not understand what is meant by a basic rhythmic cycle, begin to clap at a very slow, steady rhythm. Your clap indicates the first beat of a cycle, regardless of whether it is a cycle of one, four, or nine beats. Every first beat completes one cycle and begins the next. Now, for every clap, count out loud the beats of the rhythmic cycle. First just count one for each clap: One. One. One. Then count two beats for each clap: One, two. One, two—and so on. Continue up to nine beats, counting out nine even intervals for every one clap—making sure the intervals really are even. The length of the entire cycle should remain constant regardless of how many beats per cycle you are counting. In other words, the intervals between your claps do not increase. So in order to count nine beats per cycle, you must count three times as fast as when you were only counting three beats.

Alternatively, you can mark the basic rhythm with your footsteps: for every step, count out the beats: one, two, three, four, five, seven, or nine per step. These are the basic rhythmic cycles.

Now you can begin to play with them: you can divide the nine beats in different ways, by emphasizing certain beats such as the first and fifth, or the first, fourth, and seventh. Notice how different ways of placing the emphasis alter the feeling of the rhythm.

Hands, feet, and voice are the basic rhythmic tools of the body—drums and other percussion instruments are merely extensions of these. Certain cultures have developed highly intricate rhythmic languages, representing percussion sounds through syllables, so that entire rhythmic sequences can be played on a drum, danced, or spoken with equal ease.

You can combine different rhythms within your own body by marking one rhythm with your feet, a second with your clapping, and a third with your voice. By combining hands, feet, and voice, you have access to infinite possibilities of rhythmic play. Western music and dance tend to limit themselves to three- and four-beat rhythms, but African, Asian, and Middle Eastern music may use any number of rhythmic beats to a cycle. Many Greek, Romanian, and Yugoslav folk dances utilize five- and seven-beat rhythms. African music often overlays different cycles simultaneously to achieve complex patterns.

In South Indian dance, the seven rhythms are verbalized with the help of the following syllables:

One beat: DEI
Two beats: DEI DEI
Three beats: DA KEE TA
Four beats: DA KA DEE MEE
Five beats: DA KA DA KEE TA
Seven beats (=three+four): DA KEE TA DA KA DEE MEE
Nine beats (=four+five): DA KA DEE MEE DA KA DA KEE TA

Of course, you can choose your own sounds and syllables for the rhythms. Try playing with some unfamiliar rhythms. You will find that they evoke new movements. To find out more about any of these rhythms, begin clapping or walking while you say the syllables you have chosen, and listen carefully. Start to explore a rhythm that attracts you. As you speak or clap it, close your eyes. See whether you can envision any movements for it. Or just get up, move, and find out how your body wants to respond to this rhythm. You will find that each rhythm evokes a certain mood and alters your frame of mind.

The five-beat rhythm, with an emphasis on the first and third beats, is one of my favorites. Reciting the five beats, I find that the syllables of a chant arise: Ama, Heyama, Ama, Heyama, Ama Heyama. . . . In my mind's eye, I see a circle of women doing a trance dance together. The first beat is a clear swift stamp, while on the last three beats, they let their whole body fall toward the center with a circular motion of the arms.

The only way to understand rhythm is to play with it, feel it, and dance it. Rhythmic attunement is not an intellectual achievement but an organic process that unfolds in its own time; it cannot be rushed. A person must be willing to immerse herself in any given rhythm for a long period of time, until it moves and breathes through her. Only then does the spiritual power of any particular rhythm reveal itself. But don't get overly serious about rhythm! Rhythm is play and meditation at the same time. It is both entertainment and healing. The following is an example of a rhythmic game, which is fun to play alone and even more fun in groups. It is based on a four-beat rhythm:

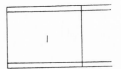

These four beats can be subdivided into sixteenths:

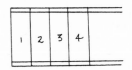

Now, take six small objects—pebbles, or grains of rice, or something else. Place one of them on square one. Place the other five randomly in any five of the other sixteen squares. Note the six numbers you have chosen. This is your rhythm! For instance, I chose the following combination:

There are many ways to play your rhythm. The easiest is the following: begin to count out loud from one to sixteen. On the six beats you have picked, add a clap. Okay? As you see, this can get quite tricky, and in a moment, it is going to get it even trickier. But first of all, keep going with your counting and clapping until you really begin to get a feel for your rhythm.

Now, add some steps! Get up and begin to walk very slowly. As you walk, take up your counting from one to sixteen again. Count out four beats for every step you take. So, you are taking a step on one, five, nine, and thirteen. When you are ready, start clapping your rhythm once again. So now, you should be walking the basic four beats, counting out sixteen, and clapping your rhythm.

As you become more sure of your rhythm, you may be able to just whisper the sixteen counts, and finally drop them entirely, just walking the four beats and clapping out your rhythm.

A well-known rhythm of this kind is the bell part that often accompanies Caribbean music. It goes like this:

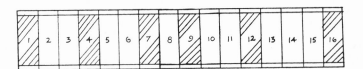 

There are endless variations to this game. You can work with words and syllables. You can find steps and songs for your rhythm, or you can drum it out. Instead of basing your game on a four- or eight-beat rhythm, you can try working with cycles of three, five, six, seven, or nine beats. If you are in a group, it is a lot of fun to subdivide the group. At first, try just two subgroups. Each subgroup will learn its rhythm separately. Then, combine the two rhythms and see what happens. Have fun!

CHAPTER EIGHT

The Art of Balance

Out beyond ideas of wrongdoing and rightdoing
there is a field. I'll meet you there.

When the soul lies down in that grass,
the world is too full to talk about.
Ideas, language, even the phrase *each other*
doesn't make any sense.

RUMI

The Path of Balance

To practice the art of balance is to unreservedly accept our physical existence. And so the Judeo-Christian traditions, and all others that consider the world a fallen place in need of redemption, have little regard for the value of balance. In that transcendent realm of pure spirit where God the father is said to reside along with hosts of angels and the souls of the redeemed, there are no opposing polarities and hence no need for balance. Instead of seeing the physical world as a practice ground for the art of balance, these cultures have relegated it to the realm of the feminine—so dangerous, so seductive, so infectiously contaminating, that any degree of involvement with it can lead to disaster and loss of soul. We see this among certain orders of Buddhist and Hindu monks, who are entirely forbidden to speak to women. Within the more ascetic branches of all major world religions, isolation, hunger, and thirst, extremes of heat and cold, sexual and various other forms of deprivation may be used to subjugate the body.

On the path of balance, however, spiritual realization is sought not in the seclusion of monastic life, but in the midst of intense activity and involvement. The medieval mystic Meister Eckhart, himself a master of balance, says:

> I have been asked the following question. Many people withdraw from the crowd and wish always to be alone, finding their peace in this and in being in church. Is this the best thing to do? I replied: No, it isn't. And this is why.
>
> For those for whom things are right, they are right in all places and among all people. But for those for whom things aren't right, they aren't right anywhere or in any company. Those for whom things are right truly have God as a companion, and whoever has God truly as a companion, is with him in all places, both on the street and among people, as well as in church or in the desert or in a monastic cell. No one can hinder the person who possesses God aright.[1]

Our quest for balance is instinctual: every child, for no apparent reason, will one day struggle to rise to a standing position and, waging a heroic battle, will rise and fall and rise again, until mastering the challenge of physical balance.

The path of balance views all aspects of life as interrelated. No aspect of life is rejected as impure or irrelevant to spiritual evolution. Buying groceries is as much spiritual practice as chanting mantras. Spiritual practice involves the transformation of both body and mind, for physical, mental, and spiritual balance are not separate but related. As a spiritual discipline, the path of balance is based on acceptance of nature, of our instincts and our body. It invites us to cooperate with ourselves as we are, instead of trying to become something different and more "pure."

Namkhai Norbu explains that while Hinayana and Mahayana Buddhism tend to consider the body as impure, Vajrayana (the indestructible vehicle) Buddhism affirms the oneness of spirit and body and accordingly attributes great importance to movement meditation:

> The relative is thus not renounced or rejected as impure, but is used as the means of transformation itself, until dualism is overcome, and all phenomena, both relative and absolute, can be said to be "of one taste"—pure from the very beginning.
>
> Thus in the Yantra Yoga of the Vajrayana, body, voice, and mind and their functions are not blocked or neutralized as in Hatha Yoga, but are accepted as the inherent qualities, or "ornaments" of the state, manifesting as energy. Since energy is continually in movement, Yantra Yoga, unlike the static Hatha Yoga, is dynamic, and works with a series of movements linked to breathing.[2]

According to Asian systems of medicine, and Tibetan and Chinese medicine in particular, balance is synonymous with health; without exception, loss of balance is considered the root cause of all disease. Because our physical, mental, and spiritual centers are interwoven, loss of balance on one level affects the entire person. It makes little sense to center yourself through spiritual practice if you avoid dealing with the mental issues that cause you to lose your balance. What is the use of feeling blissfully centered alone on a mountaintop if you begin fighting with your children as soon as you return home? We need to work on all levels at once, combining spiritual practice with physical exercise, therapy, and the processing of relationships.

When I do intensive inner work for several days, I notice a pattern. After the first day or so, my sense of balance is terrible. I feel light-headed, confused, and disoriented. Now I recognize that feeling. I am taking myself apart so that all the toxins can be cleaned out. I feel vulnerable, anxious, and emotionally unbalanced. I begin processing what emerges. After another few days, I begin to come together in a new way. I feel light, yet strong and rock-solid. My physical balance is perfect. For the time being, I rest in my center, physically, mentally, and spiritually.

The Symbol of Balance

I don't think there is any form of dance that does not incorporate the figure-eight movement. It is a movement so natural, so graceful and pleasurable that people inevitably discover it and play with it when they move. The figure-eight motion is one of the most soothing and healing movements, and many traditional trance dances are based on it. You can experience its relaxing qualities for yourself right now. Just imagine that an invisible pencil is attached between your eyebrows. Now spend a few minutes with closed eyes, breathing deeply and tracing a lying down figure eight in the air with this invisible pencil, moving very slowly. If you like, you can visualize the symbol appearing as a band of light against a deep blue sky. This simple exercise will help your eyes, forehead, and neck to relax.

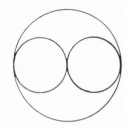

Now imagine a large circle around the figure eight, and you have what I call the *symbol of balance*.

Although the form may vary in minor ways, the symbol of balance has three main elements: a single large circle, two smaller circles, and a centerpoint.

The single circle is, according to Rumi, the field "beyond ideas of wrongdoing and rightdoing," the eternal playground of mystics. It signifies the unbroken wholeness before the fall, the sage's innocent, enlightened foolishness. The two smaller circles represent the pairs of opposites; they include the entire realm of conceptual mind as well as all the polarities and pulsations of creation.

Now notice the center of the large circle, which is also the only point where the two smaller circles meet. Like an old squabbling couple who disagree in all things and yet are joined by the deeper awareness of their love, all the opposites are reconciled in this point. This is the point of perfect balance: physical, emotional, and spiritual; the magical place we spend all our life searching, finding, and losing again.

The symbol of balance maps out the relationship of the finite and the infinite. It introduces us to the paradoxical nature of the Great Spirit, whom we may encounter both as the centerpoint in the very heart of our heart and as the infinite circumference of the universe.

Balance Is Movement

In the symbol of balance, the larger, outer circle symbolizes a motionless state. The two smaller circles that form the figure eight represent dynamic movement, the primal serpent-wave of creation itself. The cosmos retains a state of creative imbalance yet strives to achieve equilibrium, all in constant movement. With the achievement of perfect balance, all movement would cease and creation would come to an end. The Chinese yin-yang symbol (see page 136), another version of the symbol of balance, illustrates the dynamic aspect of duality as movement. It shows how all the wave pulsations of moving energy arise from the separation of the one into two.

Although oneness is a state, balance itself is never a fixed state but rather an ongoing process of awareness in motion. Even the greatest masters of balance continuously fall out of their center. The difference is that they know, in every moment, where they stand in relationship to it, and so can recenter almost immediately, whereas most of us stagger and reel like drunkards under the impact of minor disturbances and mishaps.

Imagine a tightrope walker in a circus. She constantly corrects her equilibrium as she dances across the rope, absorbed in her meditation on gravity. Like a tightrope walker, the spiritual seeker is continually drawn out of her center, and must continually refocus. The forces that distract, confuse, fascinate, and terrify us are as the pull of gravity is to the tightrope walker. We need to learn to interact with the world while maintaining our connection with stillness, and with our Hara. We need to practice, until we are able to play with the energies on both sides without falling.

Introversion and Extroversion

The symbol of balance offers a masterpiece of choreographic shorthand mapping out the dance of balance for us. When we understand the need for balance, we can let go of the belief that it is more spiritual to turn inward than to focus outward. Would we expect a bird to fly with only one wing? As you draw the balance symbol with your hands and arms, you will find that the same energy that hurls your hand outward invariably carries it back toward the center. The outward leads to the inward movement, and the inward again turns into the outward. There is a natural rhythmic pulsation of involvement and withdrawal. Philosopher Alan Watts in one of his lectures discussed this phenomenon:

> It's just like riding a bicycle. It's a balance trick. You suddenly find yourself falling over one way, well you balance that, you turn into that direction and you stay up. And so, in the same way, when you find yourself becoming too attached to life, you correct that with the realization that there is nothing except the eternal now. Then, when you feel that's all right, you see you're safe again, free of the eternal now. Once more you go and get attached, or you get involved, you get concerned about some enterprise, social, political, amorous, familial, scholarly, artistic, whatever it is, you get involved. The two always go together.[3]

You may have been told that playing with pleasure like a delighted child in a giant toyshop, is not a very "spiritual" thing to do. But if we constantly squelch our impulse to go out and play, a bleakness will overshadow our spirit. Our childlike sense of fascination with the world is so closely linked with our creative potential that to repress it is to maim the divine child within ourselves. To be sure, our desires can be obsessive and disturbing, and they are not easily controlled. But, a master equestrian does not kill an Arabian horse because of its wildness—on the contrary, he appreciates the creature all the more and works with it patiently.

Similarly, on the path of balance, we work *with* our ego, not against it. As we have seen before, the ego has its place and its function in our life, and we need not suppress it. Instead, we listen to it, honor its voice, hear its needs, and give it a space within which it can dance. Often, the ego will supply the very information we most need in order to go beyond our present limitations.

The figure-eight movement explicitly encourages you to fly off to the right and the left, and yet, it always leads you gently back to the centerpoint. It teaches you to accept yourself when your thoughts are scattered, as well as when your mind is focused. The German word *Zerstreuung* means "entertainment," but its more literal translation would be "scattering." The highest forms of theatrical entertainment, whether they be Shakespearean plays or the dramas of Balinese dance, affect us like the figure-eight movement: they take our mind and scatter it, shaking loose old obsessions. Then, they gently bring us back to our center, leaving us uplifted and relaxed. There is a great joy in discovering these two things: that it is perfectly fine to move out of our center, and that we will most certainly find our way back.

Judgment

What we perceive as pairs of opposites are opposites only within the framework of our dualistic mind. Though our perspective is limited, we form our concepts and make our judgments based upon these limitations. For example, day and night appear as opposites to us, as long as we experience them on the earth's surface. But the astronaut in outer space sees only a single revolving planet. Similarly, when the earth was discovered to be round and not flat, the relativity of directions such as east and west became evident.

The symbol of balance shows two circles within a larger circle, thus describing the relationship of reality as a whole to the dualities we perceive, all of which are relative, mutually interdependent, and contained within a greater circle of oneness. The meaning of all dualistic concepts transforms as our perspective widens; as Fritjof Capra notes:

> The original meaning of the words *yin* and *yang* was that of the shady and sunny sides of a mountain, a meaning which gives a good idea of the relativity of the two concepts.[4]

Illuminated by the sun of our conscious awareness, the psyche also has a light and a shadowed side. Certain aspects of ourselves we accept and are conscious of, others we repress or deny. Yet both sides have equal value and both are equally essential to the wholeness of who we are. Positive and negative emotions possess equal transformative potential. With this in mind the Buddhist master Chögyam Trungpa taught his students to think of their own waste not as "shit," but as "manure," material that would help them to fertilize a magnificent garden. Similarly, Thich Nhat Hanh teaches:

> Defiled or immaculate. Dirty or pure. These are concepts we form in our mind. A beautiful rose we have just cut and placed in our vase is immaculate. It smells so good, so pure, so fresh. It supports the idea of immaculateness. The opposite is a garbage can. It smells horrible, and it is filled with rotten things.
>
> But that is only when you look on the surface. If you look more deeply you will see that in just five or six days, the rose will become part of the garbage. You do not need to wait five days to see it. If you just look at the rose, and you look deeply, you can see it now. And if you look into the garbage can, you see that in a few months its contents can be transformed into lovely vegetables, and even a rose.[5]

Tolerance is rooted in the knowledge that even our most deeply cherished beliefs, though they may have served us well, are relative. They are encompassed by a reality far more vast than our mind can comprehend. To completely identify with any concept or ideal, no matter how true it might seem, is to imprison oneself within dualism. As Lao Tsu says:

> Under heaven all can see beauty as beauty only because there is ugliness. All can know good as good only because there is evil.[6]

Judgments exist only in the mind, not in the body. For this reason, dance is one of the most powerful transformational tools we have for disengaging from the judgmental mind. Dance leads us out of judging mind into immediate, nonconceptual experience. As we dance, we enter a universe in which all emotions and thoughts are perceived as moving energy patterns. Anger might appear as a fiery swirling cloud, peace as a silent blue lake.

The great traditions of spiritual dance are based upon the understanding that no aspect of life, or of the human psyche, is unworthy of being danced as an offering to the divine. Hate, jealousy, anger, pride, and possessiveness are as worthy of expression as are love, joy, tenderness, and beauty.

An ancient Hindu myth describing the first dance performance expresses the human need to transcend the limitations of moral judgment. The dance performance, it is said, took place not on earth, but in the heaven of the sky god Indra. The musicians who played for the dancers were themselves gods, and the dancers no ordinary mortals, but celestial beings of radiant beauty and grace.

Nevertheless, events did not run quite as smoothly as anticipated. In the middle of the festivities, the demons suddenly stormed into the court and rudely interrupted the performance. The dance, they complained, was unfair to them. The gods were being honored as good and great. No one could watch the drama without being moved by their heroic deeds, generosity, and wisdom. The demons on the other hand had been completely excluded, their very existence ignored, and this, they protested, was unfair.

The gods were forced to admit that this criticism was indeed valid; when planning the performance, they had judged the demons and their activities unworthy subject matter for such a lofty spiritual art, performed for so exalted an audience.

But, as the demons pointed out, their function in the maintenance of the universe was, in all ways, of equal importance to that of the gods. For without the demonic contribution, no one would understand the true meaning of beauty and goodness. Without the blackness of charcoal, the diamond's sparkle could not be appreciated, and without the evil of the demon race, the radiance of the gods would have no meaning. And so the demons demanded equal honor and status in the dance.

And so it happened: thereafter, the dance was performed as an expression not merely of the "good" point of view, but of reality in all its aspects, good and evil, beauty and ugliness. And since that time, no dancer is considered accomplished in the art unless he or she can dance the part of both god and demons: both Rama, god on earth, as well as the part of Rama's foe Ravana, the great ten-headed demon; the part of Sita, the enchanting goddess, as well as of Putana, the demon who tried to suckle the divine baby Krishna with her poisoned breast.

With gentle humor, this tale chides the organizers of the dance performance for their fanatical support of the gods. In any conflict, to identify exclusively with one side, rather than with the whole, is to open oneself to fanaticism. Parallels to the story of the excluded demons can be witnessed among the innumerable political struggles presently consuming humanity. Here each side thinks of itself as the champion of goodness and considers its enemies demonic. In such conflicts, we identify with our own values so completely that we become incapable of recognizing both the necessity and value of the opposing standpoint.

This does not mean that one's beliefs must be surrendered; moral and ethical judgments are necessary and useful. The gods are not asked to approve of the demons, nor are the demons asked to become more godlike. But if both are allowed to express themselves and to be heard by the other, then they can dance together.

Centerpoints

Centerpoints are gateways to infinity. Every shamanic culture knows of gateways through which one may pass from one world into another. As we have seen when looking at the symbol of balance, the meeting point of the

Passageway into the inner sanctuary at the temple of Al Tarxien, Malta 2400–2300 B.C.E.

two smaller circles is also the centerpoint of the one all-encompassing circle. This point represents the gateway to infinity: *Wherever two opposites meet, such a gateway exists.* In lovemaking, masculine and feminine energies meet, and therefore sexuality can function as another entrance to the transcendent.[7] Night and day converge at dawn and again at dusk—in all shamanic cultures these times are considered times of power, during which one may pass through into other worlds. In the *Breathwaves* meditation, we described the moment between inhalation and exhalation as such a doorway. Another such juncture is the state of consciousness between wakefulness and sleep.

But the first, foremost, and safest among the gateways to the transpersonal realm is the present moment. Behind you lies the entire past, before you the entire future. The common goal of innumerable meditation techniques is to teach you to maintain presence, catching your mind as it falls into the past and into the future, patiently returning it back to the present moment. For this practice, the Buddhist Thich Nhat Hanh teaches his students short verses of remembrance:

> Breathing in, I calm body and mind.
> Breathing out, I smile.

Dwelling in the present moment,
I know this is the only moment.[8]

The mind can only grasp time as a linear, two-way track. Through meditation, however, we discover that, sandwiched between the past and the future, the dimensionless point of NOW is limitless, unbounded by space and time that opens like a trapdoor into the depths of infinite universes.

The Shamanic Path

For most of us, balancing the dualities of daily existence is more than enough of a challenge. But another whole level of mastery is demonstrated by the shaman, who knows how to slip through the cracks between the material and nonmaterial worlds and leave the circles of duality, going entirely "beyond ideas of wrongdoing and rightdoing," and returning with the knowledge of how to live in both planes simultaneously. The shaman possesses the special ability to remain balanced on the threshold between the two worlds, voluntarily crossing over between one and the other, to bring back information and healing gifts for the benefit of humanity. The shaman is the ultimate master of the art of balance, physically as well as spiritually.

The multi-leveled nature of psychic reality parallels that of physical reality. Underlying and overlapping the familiar dimensions of daily life lie the less familiar but equally real worlds of the very small and the very large: the worlds of subatomic particles and of vast whirling galaxies. In these extreme dimensions, our usual description of certain entities as "pairs of opposites" is not valid. Here, boundaries between space and time, day and night, even between what is up and what is down, dissolve. As Fritjof Capra remarks, "in atomic physics we have to go even beyond the concepts of existence and non-existence."[9] Subatomic particles can, he claims, never be said to exist or not exist in any given moment, but can only be described in terms of oscillating probability patterns.

To become a citizen of the non-dual transpersonal universe, the shaman must allow all ordinary boundaries to dissolve within herself. Shamanic knowledge of how to cross over into this realm and return with the gift of healing is generally won through an intense process of suffering, illness or initiation. In this realm, space, time, and causation dissolve, or have a different meaning than in ordinary life. The danger of slipping and losing balance is therefore not merely a poetic metaphor, but very real: for those in pursuit of higher wisdom and power, the loss of balance can result in injury, madness, and death. Indeed, many shamans endure phases of insanity.

Most people spend their entire life within the confines of the dualistic mind, never stepping into the vast waters beyond. Or they may be thrown into that vastness involuntarily by accident, illness, drugs, or by a near-death experience. Those whom we label psychotic include people who were plunged into the non-dual realms without adequate preparation and were unable to integrate their experience. The many years of training that shamans are required to undergo serve to develop the exquisite sense of balance essential to their journeys across the boundaries. The researcher Barbara Myerhoff tells how the famous Huichol shaman Ramón Medina Silva taught her that without the mastery of balance, the shaman will inevitably fail and crash into the depths, both literally and figuratively. The shaman is nothing, if not the ultimate master of balance:

> I first became aware of the significance of the shaman's need for exquisite balance in my contact with the Huichol Indians of North Central Mexico several years ago. For some time I had been working with a Huichol *mara'akáme,* or shaman priest, named Ramón Medina Silva. One afternoon, without explanation, he interrupted our sessions of taping mythology to take a party of Huichol friends and myself, to an area outside his home. It was a region of steep barrancas cut by a rapid waterfall cascading perhaps a thousand feet over jagged, slippery rocks. At the edge of the fall, Ramón removed his sandals and announced that this was a special place for shamans. He proceeded to leap across the waterfall, from rock to rock, frequently pausing, his body bent forward, his arms outspread, head thrown back, entirely bird-like, poised motionlessly on one foot. He disappeared, reemerged, leaped about, and finally achieved the other side. I was frightened and puzzled by the performance, but none of the Huichols there seemed at all worried.

The wife of one of the older Huichol men told me that her husband had started to become a *mara'akáme* but had failed because he lacked balance. I assumed that she referred to his social and personal unsteadiness, for he was an alcoholic and something of a deviant. I knew I had witnessed a virtuoso display of balance, but it was not until the next day when discussing this event with Ramón that I began to understand more clearly what had occurred. "The *mara'akáme* must have superb equilibrium," he said and demonstrated the point by using his fingers to march up his violin bow. "Otherwise he will not reach his destination and will fall this way or that," and his fingers plunged into an imaginary abyss. "One crosses over; it is very narrow and without balance, one is eaten by those animals waiting below."[10]

The shaman's three most important vehicles of passage are narcotics, rhythm, and dance. Like shamanic drumming, described in the previous chapter, the power of shamanic dancing, which stems from its repetitiveness and monotony, entrances the linear mind.

A traditional shaman usually travels into the beyond for the sake of an individual's healing, but at times shamanic journeying might also occur on behalf of the whole community. For example, the Sioux holy man Black Elk, faced with the annihilation of his people at the hands of white settlers, began to receive visions of his people's past, present, and future path, which guided him to serve as a healer. Today, it seems that our collective unconscious is sending us, in great numbers, to make contact with the spirit worlds, since our collective need for realignment with those realms is so urgent.

Dorothy Maclean, the woman who contacted the nature spirits of Findhorn, asserted that the angels she encountered were overjoyed to find humans reaching out for communication with them, after such a long period of denial and violation of the cosmic laws they represent. Similarly, in our movement meditation groups, we often sense the presence of beings who are attracted to the circle, and quite frequently members of the circle enter states of trance in which they spontaneously undergo what is very like a shamanic journey.

Though most of us would not describe ourselves as shamans, the shaman is an archetype that we all embody at certain times in our life. Today, our collective consciousness is awakening us to the need to journey into other universes. By doing so, we awaken to the greater context within which human life is lived and realize how much depends on our willingness to live a life of balance, not just for our own sake, but for the sake of all beings.

CHAPTER EIGHT: MEDITATIONS

The Symbol of Balance

RECOMMENDED MUSIC: Meditation or rhythmic music

In the following meditations, the figure eight corresponds to the path of our movement, while the encompassing circle represents the awareness with which we meditate: the awareness of our own sanctity as a part of the whole.

The figure-eight movement is powerful medicine. It causes body and mind to rebalance and remember their original wholeness. Even if you have never done this movement before, your body already knows it. Like the memory of a language once spoken but since forgotten, it is knowledge that lies dormant within the body, waiting to be evoked.

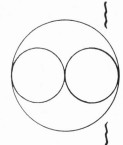

Stand comfortably, with your feet slightly separated. Make sure your knees are relaxed and unlocked. Breathe deeply. Close your eyes.

Visualize the symbol of balance. See it as clearly as possible, as if painted with bright blue or crimson paint on a large canvas. See the centerpoint and the two circles. Feel the large surrounding circle encompassing your entire body.

Keeping your eyes closed, begin to sway slowly, shifting your weight from one foot to another. As you sway, visualize the two circles, one on the right, and one on the left.

Now feel your heart-center, in the very middle of your chest. Continue to sway from side to side, visualizing the symbol of balance, until you can feel your heart-center clearly.

Now, keeping your eyes closed, raise both hands in front of you to the height of your heart. Imagine that each hand is holding a pencil or a paintbrush.

Begin to carefully draw the figure eight in the air. Start with your right hand. Moving from the center, draw a counterclockwise circle on the right and return to the centerpoint. Then, your left hand takes over

where the right left off, drawing a clockwise circle to the left side and again returning to the center.

Notice the special quality of the point where the two circles meet. Try pausing in this point for just a moment before moving on. It is a place of rest and homecoming, a place where you may encounter a sudden deep silence in the midst of your movement.

Once your hands and arms understand the movement, begin to let your whole body participate in the figure-eight movement. Your shoulders, your neck and head, your rib cage, and your pelvis all begin to respond to the flow of the movement. Keep your knees soft, so your spine can rotate in all directions.

Begin to internalize the movement, dancing it less with your arms than with your spine. When you begin to clearly feel the figure eight moving inside your body, try letting your arms and hands drop. Let the movement of balancing continue within your torso.

In the beginning, it is important that you follow the figure eight very carefully. If a paintbrush were attached to the middle of your chest, would it paint an even, rounded figure eight? Or would the figure be lopsided, wobbly?

No two people will do this movement in exactly the same way. Your way is unique, a reflection of who you are. Pay careful attention. Breathe, and be aware of the exact moment of passing through your heart-center. Notice the meeting point of your two circles, and feel this point within your body.

Pay attention to the two sides of your body. Do they feel the same, or different? Don't try to analyze or interpret your experience; simply remain receptive and observant. And breathe. Never block your breath.

Whenever you want, but especially if you lose touch of the sensation of inner movement—that is, the movement of your spine and the subtle energy within your body—return to drawing the symbol of balance with your hands.

As you move, remember that what you are now meditating on is the symbol of cosmic balance. All aspects of you are of equal value, are equally significant in the eyes of the infinite. Listen carefully within as you move, and try not to interfere. Whatever arises, let it be.

If you find now that your body wants to change the movements, allow this to happen. Let them transform. Let the dance begin. Let the figure eights move through all parts of your body, your pelvis, your shoulders, your head.

Let yourself move freely now, aware of the spaciousness and vastness within which your movements are contained. Through your body, you can open to the experience of the oneness and balance underlying all pairs of opposites.

Allow yourself to play with the movement, letting it shift, transform, and develop freely. Play with your thoughts, keeping focused and yet allowing associated images and ideas to flow through you.

Move as long as you wish.

Then sit down in a comfortable position. Perhaps you can still feel the movement continuing within you, even while you are quietly resting. Watch your breath as it flows through your center.

Feel the breath flowing through you. Feel the two sides of your body, the right and the left, different yet harmonious. Rest in the centerpoint.

Be at peace with yourself.

Moving with the Breath

Sit down.

With your hands, draw the symbol of balance as described above. Now, coordinate the rhythm of your breath with your movements, so that every downward slope of the figure eight is an exhalation and every upward slope an inhalation.

Thus, with each exhalation you cross over from one hand to the other.

With the first exhalation, surrender your entire past into the present moment.

With the second exhalation, surrender your entire future into the present moment.

For at least ten minutes, continue breathing and moving in this way, surrendering your past and your future into the present moment.

The Balancing Walk

RECOMMENDED MUSIC: Silence or soft meditation music

This meditation combines three elements: a step, an arm movement, and a breathing pattern.

THE STEP: Stand on your left foot, keeping your knee very slightly bent. Slowly raise your right foot and cross your right ankle just over your left knee. Align your body and settle into this position until you feel centered in it.

Now lower your right foot again and step forward onto it. Raise your left foot to just over your right knee, again keeping your right leg slightly bent. Find your balance, and breathe gently.

THE ARM MOVEMENT: Begin with your palms joined near your heart, as for prayer. Let both your hands move downward, out, and around, describing two wide circles to the right and left, coming up and over and returning to the heart, palms once again joining.

Be aware of the balance between the two sides of your body, and the two circles. Feel your body and mind centering themselves as you join your palms.

THE BREATHING PATTERN: First, try the combination of the step and breathing. Move into the beginning position with your right foot raised. Holding this position, inhale deeply, and exhale deeply. Be sure to breathe slowly and naturally.

Inhaling, step onto your right foot.

Exhaling, lift your left foot to your right knee.

Inhale and exhale, holding the position.

Inhale and step onto your left foot.

Exhale and raise your right foot to your left knee.

Inhale and exhale, holding the position.

Keep repeating this pattern.

THE COMBINED MOVEMENT: When you feel ready, combine all the elements: Move into the beginning position with your left foot slightly raised, palms joined. Keep your palms joined as you inhale, stepping forward onto the left foot, and exhale, lifting your right foot and crossing the ankle over your left knee.

Holding the position, inhale while your arms move down and out. Exhale while they complete their circles and your palms come together again.

Keep your palms joined as you inhale, stepping forward onto the right foot, and exhale, lifting your left foot.

Holding the position, inhale while your arms move down and out. Exhale while they complete their circles and your palms come together again.

Make sure your face remains relaxed and soft as you practice. Repeat until the movement flows naturally, and you gain a sense of peaceful balance.

CHAPTER NINE

Relating to Earth

Be at one with the dust of the earth.
This is primal union.

LAO TSU

Blessed are the men and women
who are planted on your earth, in your garden,
who grow as your trees and flowers grow,
who transform their darkness to light.
Their roots plunge into darkness;
their faces turn toward the light.

ODES OF SOLOMON

The Art of Walking

I REMEMBER, in the cool of the evening time, walking down a street in Bangalore, a city of two million people in Southern India. On the corner, a girl from the slum shacks nearby squats on the sidewalk. Before her lies a piece of cloth; she has spread garlands of white jasmine flowers upon it, each tiny fragrant blossom strung and knotted carefully into place. Recognizing me, she laughs and waves, green and gold glass bangles shimmer on her dark brown arm. A woman stops, hands her a coin, and receives a piece of flower garland: from the fingertips to the elbow and back is the measure. The woman, her black braid shiny with fresh coconut oil, fastens the perfumed blossoms in her hair, and walks on.

The gait of these Indian women will stay with me forever, along with the sweet fragrance of jasmine in their hair. Though they are city women, they walk as their sisters in the country do: with dignity and ease, their feet familiar with the earth, unhurried and sure of themselves. They radiate feminine power, the relaxed kind of power that translates into a slow grace. They are not sexual objects, their sexuality is hidden, never on view to the public. Visible is their strength, their groundedness, their competence in dealing with all matters of earth, a competence won over thousands of years. Watching them, I remember a Native American chant:

> In a sacred way I walk.
> In beauty's way I walk.
> In a sacred way I walk this earth.

Many of us turn to spirituality because we find life on earth so uncomfortable and painful and would like to find a way out. Yet true spiritual practice does not concern itself with leaving the earth, but rather with the art of living here consciously and skillfully. The Tibetan Buddhist spiritual teacher, Chögyam Trungpa, says:

> The boddhisattva's discipline is to relate to earth properly, to relate to his senses and mind properly. He is not concerned with psychic phe-

nomena or other worlds. Ignoring earth to chase after psychic phenomena is like the play of children trying to find gold at the end of a rainbow. We do not have to concern ourselves with the cosmic world, the world of gods, psychic powers, angels and devils. To do so may be to lose track of the physical world in which we live, and this results in madness. The test of the boddhisattva's sanity is how directly he relates to earth. Anything else is a sidetrack.[1]

The earth Trungpa refers to here is not merely the physical planet. Earth, in this context, is the very ground of our being, that which supports us in the most basic ways. Relating to the earth is relating to reality as it is, not as we imagine it or would like it to be. Though relating to earth is the most basic practice of all, it is also the most difficult. After all, the human race would not be handling the task so poorly were there no major difficulties involved. We seem to get caught up in the illusion of our own species as separate from the fate of the rest of the earth, and we tend to think that, because human beings possess certain unique abilities, we somehow stand

The feet of God, with symbols indicating the points at which subtle energy flows enter and leave the body. India, 18th century.

apart from and above all other creatures. In fact, we are merely one organ in the body of the planet.

Gravity

The most direct way of relating to the earth is through the pull of gravity. Your weight reminds you that you are an embodied being, like a piece of heavy clay. Every time you consciously surrender to gravity, you practice the art of dying, of returning your body to the earth.

Gravity is one manifestation of the power that holds the universe together; it lets you know that you belong here. Your body may contain molecules of mountains and dinosaurs and nameless creatures of the sea. If you think of the earth as mother, then you can experience gravity as her expression of love for you. Next time you lie down, imagine being gently received and embraced, and, releasing your weight, surrender your mind, too. Feel the relief of simply being and lying peacefully on the earth.

Gravity's Opposite

We have no word for the counterpart to gravity, the force that causes flowers, trees, and human beings to grow upward, toward the sky. Yet these two forces belong together like night and day. In movement meditation, you will experience both the downward pull of gravity and the upward flow of energy through your body.

This upward flow relates to the innate urge of every creature to grow, expand, and evolve. If gravity echoes death, its counterpart expresses the urge to be born, to come into light. In physical terms, evolution has caused humans to raise themselves to the upright, standing position; spiritually, the evolutionary force fuels our yearning for enlightenment. Indian philosophy symbolizes this upward rising energy as a round disk of light called the *sudarshana chakra*. This wheel of light represents the primal substance of the universe, the light-force of which the sun is merely a minor physical manifestation. Since our body is a microcosmic version of the universe, the same disk of light also manifests within our body as the *thousand-petaled lotus,* the energy vortex located in the crown of the head. Just as cosmic light draws creation skyward, so within the human body, this highest energy vortex attracts the serpentine energy, Kundalini, and pulls it upward.

What happens, then, when the upward, assertive movement is valued, but the downward, surrendering movement is suppressed? The answer is written upon our bodies, especially upon the bodies of men who have been subjected to military training. The military posture, with its unnatural contraction of the belly and inflation of the chest, forces the body to hold a rigidly upright position and suppresses any tendency to surrender to gravity. After all, a soldier is not supposed to surrender to anything, not even the earth. Yet when the downward flow of energy is denied, the complementary upward flow is also blocked. Willpower alone maintains the appearance of uprightness, but the inner experience of a natural, skyward flow that effortlessly holds the body upright is missing.

Many people have painful back problems and bad posture due to insufficient exercise and years of sitting in chairs. But our bad backs and posture cannot simply be reduced to a question of muscular strength. At a deeper level, our relationship with earth and sky is out of kilter, and so we have lost touch with the energy flows that hold our bodies in the correct position. Whenever you habitually force yourself to "hold life together," and deny your need to surrender and collapse, the upward and the downward energy flows of the body become imbalanced. Learning to be aware of these primal energy flows and reconnect with them is the first step to developing better posture and strengthening the back. Like a battery, your body needs to make proper contact with the positive and the negative poles, with earth and sky, in order to be charged with energy.

Slowing Down

In order to regain our connection to earth we need to slow down. We need to step back from the beliefs that relentlessly drive us: the belief that we need to improve ourselves and our lives, the belief that there is not enough to go around, the belief that without tangible achievements we will be failures, and so on. As long as we allow ourselves to be driven by fear, there is no chance of discovering our own inner rhythms.

The reason we need to slow down is not that speed is wrong. The real issue is not one of speed or slowness, but that we are out of touch with the innate rhythms of nature. Our body and mind, like everything else in nature, have their own rhythms, their own ways of moving. Without knowing these rhythms, how can we chose to respect them? Slowing down is essential as a means of discovering our true rhythms.

Unlike animals—who move quickly when hunting or fleeing from danger, but relax and slow down immediately afterward—many people live in what their bodies perceive as a permanent state of alarm, until they break down with fatigue or disease. When we recognize this in ourselves, we need to make a conscious effort to break out of this cycle—and to pull the brakes. Unfortunately, many currently popular forms of exercise merely reproduce the frantic tempo of urban life. As much as we need exercise, we also need to practice moving and thinking at a speed that allows us to feel peaceful and grounded. I have found that the surest sign of alignment with my inner rhythms is a sense of gratitude for the precious gift of life, which dissipates whenever I try to push and rush.

Industrial society has become increasingly unhealthy and alienated from the whole of life. Instead of walking through the healing smells, sounds, and sights of nature, as men and women have done for thousands of years, people get in their cars and rush through a nightmare of concrete buildings and thoroughfares. Having switched from walking to driving, we are now utterly dependent on automobiles. Indeed both figuratively and literally, we are driven.

At first, the ability to move at high speeds and accomplish tasks efficiently seems—like many luxuries—a great improvement on nature; later it becomes a compulsion and a form of bondage. It is a vicious circle: the more pressured our lives become, the more we would like to rush through the tasks at hand, and the more we rush, the more ugliness we create. Ironically, the outcome is a gargantuan traffic jam that forces us to slow down and contemplate the very ugliness we would much prefer to ignore. If cities offer any indication of the level of evolution and the standard of living a society has achieved, then it must be said that modern industrial society, all over the world, is utterly barbaric. Until we begin to create environments that reflect peace, beauty, and respect for nature, our society will continue to be poor in a very fundamental sense.

The ugliness of industrial landscapes and the speed of urban life are related, for they are both expressions of fear. To blame "technology" is a mistake, because technology itself is merely a set of neutral tools. Technology becomes problematic because of the basic attitude of fear in which it is developed and applied—a symptom of the lack of spiritual connectedness from which Western industrial society suffers. When this inner poverty is projected outward, we begin to perceive the world as a dangerous place where we must fight ruthlessly to survive. Once we lose our bond with nature both within and without, all our actions radiate this imbalance. Beauty, on the other hand, is the natural expression of a sense of spiritual fullness and wholeness. When we feel in harmony with life, everything we do and create radiates beauty. Beauty affirms who we truly are and gives us a form of spiritual nourishment we need as desperately as food and drink.

The next time you are caught up in a whirlwind of frenetic activity, try imagining how a wild animal might quietly observe you in its watchful, nonjudgmental way. Though it would have no understanding of your concerns and goals, it would perceive the energy you radiate. Animals recognize peace, fear, anger, and so on. Try looking at yourself through the animal's eyes. What do you see? Recently, when one of my clients did this exercise, she saw a coyote sitting peacefully in a meadow, watching her. Through its eyes, she saw the absurdity of her frenetic, anxiety-ridden behavior and began to laugh at herself. She realized that she had lost her sense of perspective and was sacrificing her inner peace to her obsessive perfectionism. Now, it was time to relax and join the coyote.

The faster we move, the less we feel, and thus we often use speed, like a drug, to escape the fear that our inner landscape might prove overwhelmingly painful or hollow. The irony is that unless we slow down and look around inside, we will never know for sure whether or not the fearful thing we are running away from is real. A client of mine who worked obsessively had to give up a high-powered lifestyle when she fell seriously ill. After a few months of working together, she told me: "You know, I was always secretly afraid that if I stopped busying myself I would have to look at *me,* and I would discover terrible things inside, and then I would *know* for sure I was unlovable and hopeless. But the opposite is happening: I am actually beginning to like myself!"

Cultivating Gentleness

Gentleness is healing. By moving in simple, slow ways, we rediscover our natural gentleness. When we hurry, our actions take on an aspect of violence that affects both ourselves and others. But when we slow down, gentleness manifests itself spontaneously. Gentleness is love in action, and is one of the fruits of movement meditation, surfacing whenever we consciously choose to move slowly and mindfully.

I learned a great lesson in gentleness from a woman who cooked for my workshops. Cooking has always been a hurdle for me, and so I tend to hurry through it and am often quite cranky by the time I finish. This woman, on the other hand, loved to cook. Watching her handling the vegetables, I was struck by the careful attention she gave to each radish, each sweet potato. Like a kitchen goddess, she seemed to float in timeless, serene creativity, and when we gathered to eat we all felt we were being nourished by her gentleness and kindness.

Walking in the Sacred Way

One of the simplest ways of slowing down is through the practice of walking meditation. Thich Nhat Hanh has written an extremely valuable *Guide to Walking Meditation,* in which he teaches us to walk with the serenity and joy of a buddha.[2] The very slowness of walking is its greatest virtue. The mind automatically adjusts to the speed of the body: as your body stops rushing, your thoughts also quieten. No matter how restless and agitated I am, I invariably slow down and begin to feel a sense of peace and appreciation for life as I walk. Walking slowly through nature, we can really appreciate our surroundings and their beauty.

Until recently, walking was our primary form of transportation. People walked every day, everywhere; walking was as basic as breathing. Though walking seems such a basic beginners' practice, the walking meditations are among the most difficult practices included in this book. This is the irony of walking: it is so simple, the simplest movement of all, and yet, if you want to walk consciously, in such a way that your walking becomes a truly sacred dance, it requires many years, perhaps even lifetimes, of practice.

One of my first experiences with dance was with a Belgian teacher, Magda Vandevalle. I will never forget how, after four days of dancing six hours a day with us, she humbled us by rolling her eyes, shrugging in desperation, and saying: "If only I could get you to really walk one single step! But no, you cannot. Even one step, you cannot walk." At the time, though I loved her, I also thought she was crazy. But now, fifteen years later, I know Vandevalle was right: nothing is more difficult than taking a perfect, complete step.

One of the reasons walking is so healing is because it gently rocks the body from side to side, and so, like the figure-eight movement, it balances the two sides of our body and mind. Why do babies love to be rocked in a cradle? Because it takes them back to the womb, where they were rocked gently back and forth with every step their mother took. Mothers know that a healthy, warm, and well-fed baby can be walked into a state of contentment when it screams. The mother's heartbeat and her walk are the first two rhythms of life.

The Pilgrimage

The pilgrimage is an ancient and universal form of walking meditation. Even today, in an age of automobiles and jet planes, some people choose to reenact their path toward the divine in the form of a walking pilgrimage. In 1981, a woman called Peace Pilgrim was killed in an automobile accident after a lifetime of walking through America for the sake of world peace. By the simple act of walking for peace, she deeply touched many thousands of people. One of the aspects of her pilgrimage she emphasized was that, because she walked in obedience to the will of God within her and not to satisfy her ego, she was able to draw on an unlimited reservoir of strength. Well into her sixties, she said:

> I usually average twenty-five miles a day walking, depending upon how many people stop to talk to me along the way. I have gone up to fifty miles in one day to keep an appointment or because there was no shelter available. On very cold nights I walk through the night to keep warm. . . .
>
> Once a six-foot fellow, confident he could out-walk me, walked with me for 33 miles. When he gave up, his feet were blistered and his muscles ached. He was walking on his own strength; I wasn't! I was walking on that *endless energy* that comes from inner peace.[3]

The strength of the pilgrimage derives from the fact that the pilgrim is physically enacting her spiritual journey. Such enactment affirms one's commitment and one's faith in the possibility of reaching the goal. Though the physical goal might be a place such as Mecca or Canterbury, in a sense it is quite irrelevant whether the pilgrim ever reaches her physical destination, for the spiritual goal—God, enlightenment, truth, or whatever we choose to call it—has no temporal or spatial dimension. This awareness of paradox causes a shift in consciousness: the process of walking in a sacred way becomes as important as reaching the destination. For the pilgrim, the act of walking itself *is* the prayer, the meditation.

Process and Goals

The issue of pilgrimage reveals the importance of the right relationship between goal and process. Goal and process are part of every action. Process is what is happening here and now. Process is *how* you are reading this book, *how* you are breathing while you read, *how* you hold yourself. Process is always present. Goals, on the other hand, relate to purpose and the future: always, the goal is elsewhere, ahead of us in time or space. Nonetheless goals are also real and present, insofar as they determine our present consciousness.

Our ego strives to make life as pleasant as possible. It perceives the natural conditions of life as harsh, painful, and uncomfortable, and would like to improve them; the majority of our goals stem from this drive. In the past, only the very wealthy and powerful had the means of acting on their ego's material desires. Now, owing to modern technology, millions of people own luxuries such as dishwashers and automobiles. But at what cost? In just one hundred years, we have used more of the earth's resources and destroyed more plant and animal species than all the people before us did in hundreds of thousands of years. Lao Tsu's haunting words from the sixth century B.C.E. directly address the children of the twentieth century:

> Do you think you can take over the universe and improve it?
> I do not believe it can be done.
>
> The universe is sacred.
> You cannot improve it.
> If you try to change it, you will ruin it.
> If you try to hold it, you will lose it.[4]

As as result of our failing to appreciate process and overvaluing goods instead, daily life is being drained of beauty while these products—and the poisons that result from their manufacture—pile up around us. We are witnessing Lao Tsu's prophesy come true as our "improvements" threaten to ruin the planet.

Movement meditation helps us detach from the pressure of purposeful activity, teaching us to pay attention to process, to *how* we do what we do. This discipline has no goal beyond that of opening to what *is,* and becoming aware. Naturally, we can attach a purpose to the practice, such as the intention of becoming more peaceful, or healthier, but then in a sense we miss its greatest gift, the ability to simply *be.* Meditation allows us to experience movement as it arises spontaneously out of the process of being. Such movements blossom like a flower out of stillness, manifesting our soul's ecstasy and our body's wisdom.

As we have mentioned, when we practice walking meditation, where we are headed does not matter. What matters, is *how* you walk. When Zen monks practice walking meditation, they are not directed toward any geographic place. They are simply paying attention to the process of walking, simply observing their relationship to the earth. You begin by taking peaceful, aware steps for just a few minutes every day, and you may well find that these are the most enjoyable steps you take all day.

The footpath is the most basic image representing life's journey. Walking is the prototype of goal-oriented movement, the most ancient and universal of all purposeful activity. If you can learn to walk in a sacred way, you can learn to live your entire life in a sacred way. Thich Nhat Hanh writes in his *Guide to Walking Meditation:*

> What activity is most important in your life? To pass an exam, get a car or a house, or get a promotion in your career? There are so many people who have passed exams, who have bought cars and houses, who have gotten promotions, but still find themselves without peace of mind, without joy, and without happiness. The most important thing in life is to find this treasure, and then to share it with other people and with all beings. In order to have peace and joy, you must succeed in having peace within each of your steps. Your steps are the most important thing. They decide everything. I am lighting a stick of incense and joining my palms together as a lotus bud to pray for your success.[5]

Heaven and Earth

RECOMMENDED MUSIC: Meditation music

This meditation centers on the upward and the downward flows within your body. It is best practiced after you have warmed up and danced for a while.

You may notice that the downward pull seems much stronger than the upward pull, that your body wants to stay on the earth for long periods of time while moving upward seems tedious. If so, you have probably forced yourself to stay erect at times when you really wanted to collapse, and to keep going when you really needed rest. For now, respect your need to surrender to gravity. Stop making efforts of any kind and let go. Let your body determine what feels best; don't push it. When it is ready, it will move—until then, let it be. Only after you have surrendered, both physically and mentally, will you experience an upward flow of energy, your spine supported by a power other than that of your will.

Stand with both feet comfortably planted on the ground.

Gravity gently pulls at your body, tugs at your arms, your fingers.

Notice that. And be aware of how your head rests on your neck, on your shoulders, the pelvis receiving the weight of the upper body, a miracle of balance, through the thighs, knees, calves, into the feet. All your weight resting on those two feet. Toes spread, gripping the earth.

And still the downward pull does not stop at the surface of the earth, but continues. Allow roots to grow out of the soles of your feet, anchoring you firmly. Through layers of soil, gravel, rock, penetrating downward, into the earth's womb of molten rock and fire. Drop your roots until they reach the center of the earth.

In the center, all is stillness, silence. No up, no down. No pull in any direction. Having touched on that center in your mind's eye, allow your body to surrender to the pull—ever so slowly, ever so gently. First, only a slight giving in the knees, in the shoulders. Hundreds of muscles that have learned how to hold your body upright are now letting go, relaxing so slowly that it might seem nothing at all is happening.

Give yourself time to feel the process, explore the sensation of surrender. Notice all the places where the letting go is happening—in the back of the neck, the eyes, the small of the back. Encourage those muscles to release, even those that have almost forgotten the possibility.

Gently, gently begin the slow process of dropping toward the earth.

Your face is letting go, even your eyeballs are letting go, relaxing. Your knees bend, your hands reach for the earth.

And very gently, very slowly, let your body sink to the ground completely, as if into the earth's embrace. Trust your body's own unique way of surrendering. You find new points of contact—your hands, arms, knees, each letting go into the earth's firmness, into her reliability and stability.

Even when you are finally lying on the ground, the letting go does not cease. Let yourself melt, sinking deeper, letting your weight spread over the ground just a little more. Take on the heaviness and surrender of a large, contented cat. No holding back at all.

And when you think you have reached the limit, go a little further, letting your breath sink down, giving itself to the earth. Breathe out your heart, breathe out your belly.

Fully let go. Give away your body with unreserved generosity.

Let yourself rest. Feel the luxury of just resting. No need to move, no need to think, nothing to do. Only letting go into deeper and deeper silence. Letting yourself die into the earth. Exhale yourself into the earth, and inhale the earth into you, until you feel that you are one.

As you lie on the earth, be aware that you are lying on the bodies of billions of plants, animals, and people who lived on her, and died back into her soil.

Tune into her vast consciousness, into her peacefulness and abundance. Enjoy the sense of having surrendered all responsibility, all need to know. Enjoy the darkness.

Let go. Let go completely.

As exhalation naturally turns into inhalation, so the time comes naturally that your attention turns from the earth below to the space above you. That space, that light begins to call you. It touches your back gently, reminding you.

This touch too, has a power, a pull. Gently, it begins to pull your body upward. Its power is equal to that of gravity—you might call it the gravity of lightness.

This power is all around us. Every plant, every flower, every tree defies the pull of gravity and grows upward, into the sky, into the light, into space.

When you start to become aware of this force, it may feel like a tingling along your spine, or at the back of your neck. It may feel as if the sky were an expansive vacuum gently drawing you toward it.

Feel the gentle tugging, pulling upward at the nape of your neck. Follow this upward flow now, give in to it. Effortlessly allow your body to enter the upward flow, moving gently toward the open sky, muscle by muscle responding easily, nourished by this skyward energy. Allow yourself to be drawn up into either a standing or a kneeling position, whichever you prefer.

Set aside your conscious mind and your willpower. Simply surrender to the upward flow of energy. There is no effort involved. Let yourself be drawn upward easily, joyfully. Let go into the upward flow.

Your arms, too, slowly are being pulled up toward the light, your face lifting to the sun. Like a sunflower, turn toward the sky, defying gravity.

Above you is infinite freedom. Above you are endless realms of light and joy. Touch the light with your fingertips. Touch upon your limitlessness, your freedom. Until like a sunflower, you are fully opened to the sky. The light pouring down upon you is abundant, a waterfall pouring down on your head, over your fingertips, your hands and arms.

Open your body to the light, invite it inside too: light pouring through each breath, trickling down your throat, filling heart, belly, thighs. Take in as much as you can hold, nourishing yourself with light until you are fulfilled, satisfied, intoxicated with light.

Then, heavy with all the light you have absorbed, surrender again to your own weight, to the pull of gravity.

Your arms will start to feel heavy. Let go of them slowly.

Prepare yourself to give all the light and energy you received from above back into the darkness of the earth. Do not hold on to whatever you received. Pour it out, back into the earth, emptying yourself once again.

Following the body's rhythm now, moving between earth and sky. Like a hollow container, you are now empty, now full. All that remains is the tide of light and darkness sweeping through you, at its own speed, its own rhythm.

Navajo sand-painting mandala used for healing rituals.

Blessing of the Four Directions

RECOMMENDED MUSIC: Practice this meditation without music, or use your own drums and rattles.

Traditionally, the earth is blessed and sanctified before performing almost any ceremony or a ritual. This is not because the earth needs purification, but because we are in need of reestablishing our relationship to the earth. The following practice is a simple blessing of the four cardinal directions. It can be used on its own, or as a preliminary practice in conjunction with other meditations or rituals.

Your intention in this meditation is to sanctify the space around you and align yourself with the spirit of the four directions, so that no matter where you go, you are in harmony with the earth and your movements carry an awareness of moving through sacred space. You can also use this meditation to sanctify certain areas in your home or your workplace. Throughout the meditation, it is important that you breathe through your movements, and that you *move very slowly.*

Begin by turning to the East.

You are facing the direction of the rising sun, of youth, and of the spring season, the source of new growth and creative inspiration. As you stand and breathe, sense what the East means to you.

Rest both hands on your heart for a few breaths. Then slowly bring them straight forward, feeling the opening of your heart into the world. As you do so, open yourself to the possibility of new birth and new growth in all areas of your life.

When your arms are stretched straight forward, open them to the sides, like an opening flower. Doing so, feel the openness of your heart. Breathe through the softness of your heart and belly. In this moment, surrender all concern about the future. Come fully into the present moment and feel that within you which has remained trusting and open to experiencing the freshness of life.

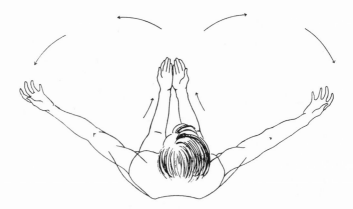

And gently bring your hands back to your heart. Feel: you are returning to yourself, coming home, greeting yourself.

This movement is repeated three times very slowly, with constant awareness of the breath, and with an attitude of receptivity to the spirit of the East.

Now place both palms together and inwardly give thanks for the blessings of the East.

Turn to the South.

The South is the direction of the midday sun that shines down from straight overhead. It is the direction of summer and rapid growth, the season of coming into adulthood and into your full power on all levels.

Drop your arms. Fingers pointing down, place your palms together. Feel the base of your spine, where it receives the earth's energy. Like a plant draws up the sap, imagine yourself drawing up earth energy through your spine. Very slowly, raise both hands from the base of your spine straight up through your center. When you reach the heart area, your fingers will automatically turn and point upward.

Move upward, until your arms are reaching into the sky, offering yourself, all that you are, into the light. Give yourself unreservedly to the light, like a sunflower turning its face to receive the sun.

Imagine light pouring down on you and, with your arms, reach for it with your entire being.

Move very, very slowly, breathing through your movements, so that you can follow the flow of energy within your body.

Breathe until your body is completely filled with light.

Then slowly, open your arms to the sides. As they drop they will feel heavy, like ripe fruits falling from a tree. Do not hold on to the light you receive: give it back to the earth. Let it drip down, oozing out of the tips of your fingers. Make sure your arms and hands relax com-

pletely. When you think they are relaxed, take a deep breath, and, as you exhale, feel them becoming even heavier.

Repeat the movement three times, opening yourself to the power of the South. Then place your palms together and give thanks to the power of the South.

Turn to the West.

This is the direction of the setting sun, of middle age, of harvest and increasing receptivity. Breathe, and feel what the West means to you.

The movement you will now do is the reversal of the movement you did facing the East.

Again, lay your hands upon your heart. From your heart, let your arms slowly reach out to the sides. Feel your willingness to be the receiver of gifts, of love, of abundance. Imagine that all you desire, and more, is spread out before you like a feast.

And in a gesture of gathering in this abundance of your life, let your hands and arms come forward and toward each other.

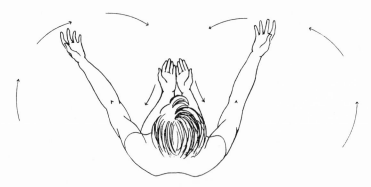

Feel all the different forms of riches you have been blessed with, and be willing to receive even more. Invoke the presence of the feminine aspect of the divine: the loving mother who blesses you with fulfillment and abundance.

When your arms are stretched straight forward, pull them inward, into your heart. Take in the satisfaction, the nourishment, the sense of fulfillment. Breathe it in deeply.

Repeat this movement three times with an attitude of receptivity to the spirit of the West. Let your body and mind join in prayer to the power of the West.

End, as before, by laying your palms together and giving thanks.

Turn to the North.

This is the direction of winter, of letting go and surrendering into the stillness of the earth. Feel the presence of darkness not as an enemy, but as a friend. North is the direction that reminds us that death is merely a preparation of the soil for new growth and rebirth. Only by dying to the past can you start fresh in every moment. The North is the direction of old age, of transformation that occurs in the depths of our being. Such transformation may not be immediately apparent, but it is nonetheless real.

The movement is as you did facing South, but in reverse.

Let your arms drop. Now, allow them to rise out to the sides, palms facing upward, moving slowly into the sky. Thus, you are encompassing your whole life, everything you have ever experienced. You are gathering in your life-force, gathering in all that you have. Continue until your hands meet overhead.

Having gathered in everything you consider yours, are you willing to let it go? To release it completely?

From straight above, let your arms slowly sink all the way down through your center. Feel everything within you relaxing, letting go,

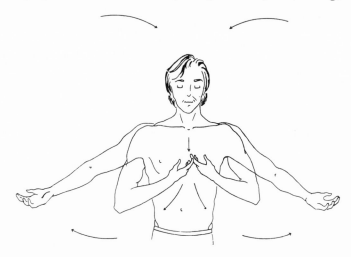

surrendering downward, into the darkness of the earth.

Repeat this movement three times, always following your breath and moving very slowly.

Feel the power of the North. Finish by thanking the spirit of the North for its gifts, as you did the other directions.

Complete the circle by turning once again to the East, where you began the meditation. Take a minute to breathe, and to feel the fullness of the circle with its four directions as it surrounds you. Feel the sky above you, and the earth below.

Say to yourself:

I am standing in sacred space. Within my body is sacred space, and around me is sacred space. My spine is aligned with the axis of the universe, the still center of all that is. May all my movements be in harmony with the spirit of East, South, West, North, the sky, and the earth. May I walk in peace upon the earth.

Upbeat and Downbeat Walk

RECOMMENDED MUSIC: Practice the upbeat and the downbeat walk without music first, then with rhythmic music.

There are many ways to practice walking as a meditation. But first I would like you to understand the two basic ways of walking, which I call the upbeat walk and the downbeat walk.

Walking is one of the most important wave movements of the body. If you imagine that your head had a paintbrush attached to it, then as you walked, you would paint waves in the air. At first, try to walk slowly and exaggerate the wave by bending your knees a little more than you normally would. Walk like this until you can clearly sense your body rising and falling with the wave. Now as you walk, pay attention to the precise moment that your foot touches the ground. If you were to draw a wave, where would you put a mark indicating a step? If you walk like most Western people, chances are your diagram would look something like this:

In this case, you are doing the downbeat walk. Your foot touches the ground as you descend into the valley of the wave. On the other hand, some people will find themselves doing something that would look like this:

This is the upbeat walk. You are placing your foot down as your head moves upwards. You may feel as if you are pushing yourself up with your step. Some people will find this movement very obvious and natural, while others may take weeks, months, or years to learn it.

The motion of walking is so complex that, as yet, no robot has been designed that could duplicate it. Hundreds of muscles are used in walking—not only the muscles in your hands, feet, and legs, but throughout your spine, shoulders, and whole body. Walking feels deceptively simple; actually, it is a movement far too complex to describe accurately on paper. These instructions can merely point the way.

For those who have difficulty finding the upbeat walk, I will outline some preliminary movements that may help you. If you already understand the upbeat walk, these steps will be unnecessary.

One trick that may help you get the hang of it is to go to a staircase, and walk down the stairs. This is the downbeat walk. Now walk up the stairs again. This is the upbeat walk. Whenever you feel unclear about either one, just imagine yourself walking up and down some stairs.

First, try walking in place with the upbeat walk. Stand, and begin to slowly bend and straighten your knees. Place the emphasis of your movement on the upward movement, as if a surge of energy was rising up from the earth and lifting your body. Now, as you bend your knees, slightly lift one foot, and, as you begin to straighten your legs, place the foot down, using it to push your body up. So the trick in the upbeat walk is to put your foot down as your body is moving up. Make sure your foot is really meeting the ground as your body moves toward the crest of the wave. Walk in place until you get a feeling for the upbeat walk. Practice this patiently until it feels comfortable.

Now, try moving forward with the upbeat walk. Start with small steps; keep them close together. Lift one foot as you dip down, and place it on the ground as you begin to come up. It is at this point that you may lose the correct movement if it is unfamiliar to you—often people revert back to the downbeat walk without even noticing it. Remember—if you are practicing the upbeat walk correctly, it should feel as if you are actually using the front foot to push yourself up from the ground.

Upbeat and downbeat walks are more than simply two different ways of moving. They are expressions of different modes of consciousness, different ways of relating to the world. The downbeat walk helps you get somewhere efficiently and quickly. It is a goal-oriented walk, a hardworking and very useful movement. It takes you where you want to go, and, if need be, it takes you there quickly. When you start to run, you automatically fall into the downbeat walk. Because we live in a goal-oriented culture, the downbeat walk is invariably what you will see on the streets of any Western city.

The upbeat walk, on the other hand, forces you to become aware of the *process* of walking. It will take you where you want to go, but it refuses to allow you to hurry there. It can transform your ordinary, mundane walk into a dance, and it provides the basic step for innumerable Greek and Balkan folk dances.

In all traditional, earth-centered cultures, people know how to walk and dance with the upbeat walk. Always, the upbeat walk conveys a slow grace, a sense of timelessness, of patiently walking the earth. It is the walk of women in India and Africa, who walk long distances to fetch water, and then return, gracefully balancing the filled pots on their heads. It is the walk of people who devote much time and attention to the basic processes of daily life: gathering food and water, cooking, washing clothes, raising children, preparing for and celebrating traditions and festivals.

The upbeat walk forces us to shift from goal-consciousness to process-consciousness, and it is therefore absolutely essential to movement meditation. Just as every spiritual tradition recognizes certain sounds and words as sacred and infused with divine energy, so, in the realm of movement, the upbeat walk holds extraordinary power. And just as no intellectual answer can explain why a certain sound vibration should be more potent than any other, so the profound power of the upbeat walk can only be experienced, not grasped mentally. Perhaps more than any other movement, the upbeat walk allows us to attune to the wave flow of our body. Being able to do the upbeat walk is the first step. Then, you must move with it one hour, many hours, until you merge with it, until you and its wave are one.

With the upbeat wave, you can walk or dance in as many ways as there are moods in your day. Seemingly so simple, the upbeat walk is the ultimate key to ecstatic dance. You must feel it in your belly, in your heart, and you must be willing to surrender and let the wave carry you.

Blessing the Earth

I recommend practicing this meditation without music. It should be done with bare feet. If possible, practice outside, on grass or soft earth.

Walk very slowly in whatever way feels natural to you. Inhale as you lift your foot, and exhale as you place it on the earth. Use an entire breath cycle for each step.

At first, walking this slowly may make you feel a little wobbly and unsteady, but if you keep practicing, you will get stronger and more balanced.

Now, focus on your exhalations. As you exhale, visualize your breath dropping down through your body, down through the foot that is now firmly planted on the earth, carrying your spirit and your vibration into the earth. Don't worry if you can't feel this in the beginning. Just imagine your breath dropping into the earth.

The earth is not dead matter. She is alive, she feels you, and you can feel her. Walking on the earth, you can breathe and speak to the earth as you would with a good friend. Just as a friend listens and responds to us, so when you breathe into the earth's body, you may find her breathing back into you.

Now begin to speak to the earth as you walk. You can speak out loud, or just talk to her in your mind. Send your love into her with your exhalation. Feel your heart touching upon the heart of the planet. Say to her whatever words come to you:

Mother Earth, I love you.
Mother Earth, I bless you.
May you be healed.
May all your creatures be happy.
Peace to you, Mother Earth.
On behalf of the human race, I ask forgiveness for having
    injured you.
Forgive us, Mother Earth.

CHAPTER TEN

The Dance of Love

I played for ten years with the girls my own age,
but now I am suddenly in fear.
I am on the way up some stairs—they are high.
Yet I have to give up my fears
if I want to take part in this love.

I have to let go the protective clothes
and meet him with the whole length of my body.
My eyes will have to be the love-candles this time.
Kabir says: Men and women in love will understand this poem.
If what you feel for the Holy One is not desire,
then what's the use of dressing with such care,
and spending so much time making your eyelids dark?

KABIR
AS ADAPTED BY ROBERT BLY

The Sacred Couple

As we enter into meditation upon our bodies as sacred space, we are working toward nothing less than the healing of an ancient cultural wound that has led us to lose, among other things, our sexual integrity. Despite our religious and social conditioning many of us intuitively know that the sexual experience can be a sacred experience of divine perfection and ecstasy. Myths from around the planet confirm our intuition, holding up a mirror in which we see not our confusion, guilt, and fear, but rather our potential for wholeness. Today, as men and women struggle to redefine sexual and gender roles, these myths remind us of an ancient archetype bubbling with transformative power: that of the divine lovers. Gentle, passionate, and erotic, they challenge our staid images of the divine and shake us awake with the joyful rhythms of their dancing feet. In their embrace, all dualities unite, and the illusion of separateness gives way to the timeless dimension of wholeness.

Goddesses and gods, saints, holy women and men all elicit projection; therein lies both their strength and their weakness. Upon them, we project our own light and shadow aspects, conjuring up giant-sized flickering images of deities both compassionate and wrathful, forgiving and vengeful. We, as the creators of our gods and goddesses, bear full responsibility for their universality or lack of it. Therefore the gods we choose to pray to and worship should be projections of perfect love, not of fear and intimidation. Those people who misuse religion to justify intolerance and violence have power only insofar as others accept their false authority and their fear-based doctrines. Keeping this in mind, meditation on a deity who appears as an intimate friend or teacher, as a child, parent, or lover, presents us with a wonderful tool to clear away our emotional debris. Whatever emotional negativity we hold, in the form of fear, anger, and envy, will disturb our spiritual practice just as it disturbs our human relationships, but it can be transformed by struggling, arguing, and making love with our chosen symbol of All That Is.

Mythology would be barren without its sacred couples, all of them different manifestations of what the ancient Greeks referred to as the *hieros gamos,* or sacred marriage. Some of these pairs are gods and goddesses like Jupiter and Hera or Vishnu and Lakshmi. Some are human servants of divine will, such as Rama and Sita, or the ruling couples of ancient Egypt. One partner may be human, the other divine, as is common in Greek mythology. Many shamans, too, claim to have spirit wives, husbands, or lovers.

The sexual union of the sacred couple may take place either in the outer world or within, as in Jungian analysis, where the Other is approached as an internal figure: the animus or anima. "The God whom I love is inside," Kabir tells us repeatedly in his ecstatic poems, while Hatha Yoga aims at an internal union of opposite energy currents.

The divine lovers remind us that our love relationships can be gateways into expanded consciousness. As the moon is reflected within a dewdrop, so the vast ecstasy of the divine radiates within the sexual energy of every individual. This conscious awareness of sexuality as sacred action differentiates human love from animal love and endows it with dignity, grace, and sanctity. The same yearning for wholeness beyond the superficial fragmentation of life fuels both the sexual and the spiritual quest. Throughout human history, people have recognized sex as a facet of the cosmic love that mysteriously recreates the world in every moment; they have revered the cosmic creativity reflected within their own creative and procreative powers.

Tantra, the ancient art of using physical and sexual energies in the service of spiritual evolution, holds that male and female energies in balance cause a fusion to take place, which can launch us into sexual and spiritual wholeness. In the East, sacred dance is considered a form of Tantra that channels the body's sensual and erotic power into an ecstatic union of body and spirit. The body's vibrational frequency heightens until the dancer becomes the lover of God or Goddess; a channel through which divine energy flows into embodied form.

Given the importance of sexual equality in Tantric practice, it is not surprising that Tantric concepts and practices have been banished from Western culture for the last three thousand years. But with the flowering of a new level of equality between men and women and the current reemergence of feminine power, Tantra is beginning to return to the West. With it, sacred dance is also returning.

The Divine Lovers in the Western Tradition

The belief that sexual energy can be channeled and transformed for the purpose of spiritual enlightenment is ancient and universal, as are analogies of mystical and sexual union. Traditional Judeo-Christian religion has banished Eros from religious life. God appears as lord, king, father, and son, but never as lover; thus he has no place at his side for his consort, the Goddess. Where God the Almighty has become exclusively male, the ancient image of the Goddess is suppressed. And having lost his feminine counterpart, God becomes de-sexed, appearing as an aged, bearded father. Indeed, one of the most striking features of mainstream Christian art and literature is the conspicuous absence of any images of lovemaking or sexual expression in general. If we are familiar with the divine lovers at all, we have encountered them primarily through the sacred art of the East.

Yet despite the fact that Christian art expelled all sexual imagery at an early date, the spiritual and sexual fire of the archetypal lovers was never completely extinguished; its embers continue to radiate a subdued glow through Western thought. The writings of the Gnostics, a suppressed branch of early Christians, contain frequent references to the sacred couple. In 1945, a large body of Gnostic texts, now known as the Nag Hammadi Library, was unearthed in Egypt, where it had been buried for more than fifteen centuries. Unpublished until 1978, these texts date from around 400 c.e. In the following excerpt from *The Sophia of Jesus Christ,* one of the Gnostic manuscripts, *Sophia,* meaning wisdom, represents the feminine aspect and consort of Christ:

> The perfect Savior said, "Son of Man harmonized with Sophia, his consort, and revealed a great androgynous light. His male name is called Savior, Begetter of All Things. His female name is called 'All-Begettress Sophia.'"[1]

The Nag Hammadi Library also includes excerpts from the Gospel of St. Thomas, which relate to our concept of the inner wedding:

> Jesus said to them, "When you make the two one, and when you make the inside like the outside and the outside like the inside, and the above like the below, and when you make the male and the female one and the same, so that the male not be male nor the female female; and when you fashion eyes in place of an eye, and a hand in place of a hand, and a foot in place of a foot, and a likeness in place of a likeness; then will you enter the Kingdom."[2]

Where sacred dance flowers, there the lovers will appear; where the lovers are, sacred dance cannot be absent. And so, we find in the Acts of John the striking description of Jesus before his crucifixion, in the midst of a circle dance with his disciples. Together they sing:

> To the universe
> belongs the dancer. Amen.

> Whoever does not dance
> does not know what happens. Amen.[3]

In the fifth century, this text was condemned as heresy, as were almost all early Christian and Gnostic scriptures.

Though most Gnostic texts were destroyed, the tradition had a major influence upon medieval alchemists in their quest to obtain the *lapis philosphorum,* an elixir of immortality in the form of a stone. They believed this stone would allow them to transform base metals into gold: its creation required that feminine and masculine essences be merged within a sort of sacred mandala, the cauldron of transformation. Centuries later, Carl Gustav Jung recognized the universality and essential spiritual truth of alchemical imagery and began to apply the archetype of sexual union to the art of healing the human psyche. In Jungian analysis, the human being becomes the cauldron of transformation in which the principles of matter and spirit, male and female, are to be united.

Even within the Christian church itself, the memory of the divine lovers, and the knowledge of wholeness they stand for, was never entirely erased. The archetype remained so strong that, throughout the Middle Ages, the Virgin Mary retained many aspects of the divine consort and was often represented sitting with Christ as his queen and equal. Many a medieval Christian nun took her role as the bride of Jesus far beyond what the Church had intended, describing her imagined, romantic encounters with Jesus in sensual terms. One historical example is Mechthild of Majdeburg, who in the thirteenth century wrote: "O Lord, love me intensely, love me often and long!"[4]

The Tradition of Indian Temple Dance

Most ancient civilizations viewed sexuality and spirituality as neighboring realms—their boundary easily crossed through the vehicle of dance. One of the few traditions based on such views that has survived into the twentieth century is that of the Devadasis of India, who were both temple dancers and sexual initiators.

In her book *Wives of the God-King: The Devadasis of Puri,* Frederique Apffel-Marglin has researched and described those customs and rituals of the Devadasis' that still exist today.[5] Several traditional temple dancers are still alive; they are, however, the last of their line, unable to hand on their tradition to a younger generation for reasons we shall discuss.

Far from being an exotic anomaly, the Devadasis' way represents one among a number of similar traditions that existed in Japan, the Middle East, Egypt, ancient Greece and Rome, and other parts of Europe. Today, however, the Devadasis are the only remaining representatives of a way of life which, having existed among human beings for millennia, will soon be extinct. As such they provide us with the extraordinary opportunity to look closely at a set of spiritual concepts and practices radically different from ours, and without parallel in the modern world.

The word *Devadasi* means woman servant of God. Trained from early childhood, a Devadasi was married to God in an elaborate ceremony as soon as she reached puberty. Her duties thereafter included ritual dancing

Indian temple dance, from the Lingaraja temple in Bhubaneshwar, India.

in the temple; these dances were symbolic representations of her lovemaking with the divine, and through this communion her sexuality was made sacred. Within certain limits defined by ritual and caste considerations, she was free to take the lovers she chose. From a Western point of view, the most striking aspect of the Devadasi tradition is that her dance was equally erotic and spiritual, and that she was both a lover of God and a lover of men. The parallel between the union of spirit and body in dance, and the union of man and woman in lovemaking, therefore, was explicitly acknowledged.

The ancient origins of the Devadasis' way of life are shrouded in the mystery of early Hindu civilization. Hindu mythology holds that dance was a gift from God, taught to the people as a path to enlightenment. Two thousand years ago, Indian dance had already reached full development, according to Bharata Muni's famous treatise *Natya Shastra,* generally dated between the fourth and the first century B.C.E. Between the ninth and eleventh centuries C.E. many of the greatest temples of South India were established through the patronage of the Chola kings. These temples became famous centers of religion, philosophy, and culture, producing works of art and craftsmanship of stupendous quality. They became the homes of the Devadasis as well.

According to all accounts, the Devadasis were highly sophisticated and cultured women whose training began in childhood. Enakshi Bhavnani describes their way of life in *The Dance in India:*

> The Devadasis enjoyed a high social status and were very accomplished. They could sing, read the classics, play on a variety of musical instruments and write on philosophical subjects. . . . Their duties were to use the fan (Chamara) on the deities and to carry the Sacred Light (Kumbarti), as well as to sing and dance before the Gods when they were carried in procession. The Devadasis received a fixed salary for these religious duties. Their training in the art of the dance was very thorough; they customarily started their studies at the age of five. Tamil inscriptions mention that in the 11th century A.D., about four hundred such dancers were attached to the great Shiva temple at Tanjore, and about a hundred to the temple at Kanchipuram.[6]

Because a Devadasi embodied the Goddess, the gift of her sexuality was considered extremely auspicious, and indeed essential to the survival of the whole country, for the Goddess represented abundance, wealth, prosperity, immortality, and fertility. By the offering of the Devadasi's spiritual and sexual energy through worship, dance, and lovemaking, it was believed that the fertility of the land would be ensured. The Devadasi's dance was performed at the same time that food was offered to the gods, ritually linking sexuality, fertility, and prosperity.

These dances, sometimes performed in the presence of the public, sometimes for the deity alone, expressed the tenderness, intimacy, and ecstasy of the Devadasi's relationship to the divine. For her to have withdrawn her sexual energy from the world of men—as Christian nuns are required to do—would have been inconceivable in this tradition. For this suppression would constitute a denial of the creative and fertile energy of the Goddess, resulting in such natural disasters as drought, crop failure, and finally starvation of the people.

The nature and purpose of the Devadasi's relationships to men were clearly set apart both from marriage and love affairs as we know them. Her commitment was not so much to any individual man, but to all men as the human reflections of her divine husband, while men acknowledged her as a human representative of the Goddess. The Devadasis distinguished between two forms of love, *aiśwarjya,* which Apffel-Marglin translates as sovereignty, versus *mādhurjya* or sweetness.[7] Aiśwarjya refers to the realm of family and marriage with its concomitant social, economic, and legal ties, all of which the Devadasi renounced in order to become the lover of God. Thus her relationships had no legal basis, did not involve financial dependency, and did not lead to family life. Her commitment, on the other hand, was to live, as fully as possible, the archetypal love called Mādhurjya, a love described in the stories of the god Krishna and his consort Radha, whose relationship represented the pure sweetness of love completely stripped of any restrictions imposed by time, space, and causality.

From Priestess to Prostitute

Extraordinary as the Devadasi's path may seem to us, her challenge was that of any person deeply committed to the spiritual path: to transcend attachment, possessiveness, and self-centeredness in order to become an embodiment of pure love. Though part of a society undoubtedly cruel in certain respects, the ancient system nonetheless reflected a deep reverence for feminine power. One can imagine how utterly alien the Devadasi tradition must have seemed to India's British colonial rulers. According to the British view, a respectable woman had two options only: she could be a wife, or she could remain celibate. Anything else constituted a moral outrage. Thus the Devadasis came to be branded as prostitutes, an ironic twisting of reality considering their unusually autonomous economic status. For although the Devadasis might receive gifts from lovers, they were provided for by their temple and by the king who supported it. Some Devadasis were extremely wealthy in their own right and so, financially independent. Clearly, this system depended upon the economic and political strength of the kingdoms and the temples. As time went on, with the decline of independent kingdoms some Devadasis did indeed turn to their lovers for support. They did so, however, in the context of crisis and as a matter of survival, not in accordance with tradition. The very need to look for outside sources of income itself signifies that the social basis for the institution of the Devadasis had begun to crumble.

As a practitioner of the ancient and very beautiful art of Indian temple dance, I consider myself as belonging to the legacy of the Devadasis; while living in India, I was very interested in finding out as much as possible about their customs and way of life. But as I began to search and ask questions there, I found the topic to be shrouded in a veil of silence and denial.

One of the reasons accurate information is so difficult to find is that many of the authors who write on the subject today pride themselves on being "respectable" dancers who have completely distanced themselves from the sexual aspects of their profession. Though many Indian dancers express pride in their ancient roots, the puritanism they have adopted from the English blatantly contradicts the joyous affirmation of sensuality and eroticism of ancient Indian art.

In this century, Indians began to recognize the value of their own culture and have tried to restore it to a position of respect. But India today is a thoroughly patriarchal country, with all the symptoms of body denial and sexual repression that patriarchy engenders. Although the national dance forms have been reinstated, the dance that survives is a "purified" version and has been stripped of any movements that might possibly appear overtly erotic. Even in the laundered form in which it survives, Indian temple dance still carries the stigma of immorality. Many parents will not allow their young daughters to dance at all, and many talented dancers stop dancing as soon as they marry because of their husbands' disapproval. The nine Devadasis whom Frederique Apffel-Marglin interviewed from 1975 to 1980 are the last representatives of the sexual history of Indian dance. They have no heirs and have themselves been ostracized. As Apffel-Marglin wrote,

> The view of the devadasis as morally degenerate women, and of the royal courts and the kings as the instruments of this degeneration . . . has had a definite effect on the devadasis of Puri. The devadasis are keenly aware of the moral judgement passed on them. . . .
>
> After the take-over of the administration of the temple by the state government in 1955, the devadasis turned to the State Academy of Mu-

sic and Dance to replace the traditional patronage which they had received from the king. They applied for grants to establish a school of dance and music so that they could continue to train young girls who would follow the tradition. Their requests were repeatedly denied.[8]

Thus spirituality and sexuality have, in India, undergone an even more extreme process of fragmentation than has occurred in the West. We will never know what the ancient temple dances really looked like, but we can imagine that they combined the grace, power, and dignity of contemporary classical Indian dance with the undulating erotic movements of what we now know as Middle Eastern dance. To this day, the sculptures adorning the walls of the temples where the Devadasis danced speak of a time when men and women met in balance and harmony, celebrating a love not fragmented in body and soul.

The Legacy of Shame

Reading Apffel-Marglin's account of her discussions with the Devadasis, one is struck by the fact that an enormous burden of shame has replaced their former pride and confidence. They lack the ability to release it, having been severed from their connection with the Great Goddess. Apffel-Marglin mentions that even today, a woman who dares to engage in any kind of dance in public in the city of Puri, where the Devadasis live, may be greeted with rotten tomatoes.[9] The condemnation of the Devadasis, and of their counterparts in other cultures, reflects the powerful taboo that has descended upon all of us to prevent the merging of sexuality and spirituality. In the West also, shame and fear of harassment hold back many people who long to dance freely and expressively in public.

Shame, like a great demon, guards the threshold between the sexual and the sacred, and must be banished before we can pass into the field of unfragmented loving. Our culture devalues the feminine and all things associated with it. Thus our experience of the body, which has been assigned the feminine gender, is inherently tinged with shame. The negation of the feminine has many other side effects; one example is the exaggerated fear of obesity that plagues Western women. Another is the fact that rape victims so often feel guilt and shame over the violence committed against them. The act of rape exposes a woman's sexuality, and in our culture this sexuality remains strongly connected to shame.

Our sense of shame is directly related to the denial of the goddess who stood for the sacredness of nature and of the material world. As cultural historian William Irwin Thompson describes, the degradation of feminine sexuality under patriarchy is a process that passes through four stages or ages:

> The first age is the age of the Great Goddess; next comes the age of the temple priestess, then of the sacred temple prostitute, and finally of the entirely secular street walker. As the power of man gains in ascendancy, the religious power of woman declines. First there was a *hieros gamos,* a sacred intercourse of fertility and the storehouse in which a woman played the role of the goddess. Then there were sacred temple prostitutes who spread the ritual from the one to the many, but in that routinization of charisma the sacred meaning was lost, and the common prostitute became the totally secular figure who haunted the subculture of men. In the *diminuendo* of the movement from priestess to prostitute we see described a process of increasing urbanization and secularization in a new world in which the old universal religion of the Great Goddess is forgotten.[10]

Thompson's theory is fully supported both by archaeological evidence and by the history of our language, which reflects various layers of changing attitudes toward the feminine. The Devadasis, like all the other temple dancers, came to be described derogatorily as "whores." But as Barbara Walker informs us in *The Woman's Encyclopedia of Myths and Secrets,* even this word originally had holy, not cursed, connotations:

> Dancing harlots came to be called Hours: Persian *houri,* Greek *horae.* Egyptian temple-women also were Ladies of the Hour. Each ruled a certain hour of the night, and protected the solar boat of Ra in the underworld during his passage through her hour. The Dance of the

Hours began as a pagan ceremony of the Horae (divine "Whores") who kept the hours of the night by dances, as Christian monks later kept the hours of the day by prayers. The oldest authentic Hebrew folk dance is still called *hora* after the circle dances of the sacred harlots.[11]

Our very language betrays us when we try to speak of the crossroads of sexuality and spirituality formerly marked and celebrated by sacred dance. For instance, Nancy Qualls-Corbett's book *The Sacred Prostitute* was written with a clear awareness of the need to reintegrate sexuality as a sacred art, and yet the very title itself serves to perpetuate old misconceptions.[12] Others like Merlin Stone object that we continue to use the term "prostitute" to refer to holy women who practiced lovemaking as a sacred art:

> Women who made love in the temples were known in their own language as "sacred women," "the undefiled." Their Akkadian name of *qadishtu* is literally translated as "sanctified women" or "holy women." Yet the sexual customs in even the most academic studies of the past two centuries were nearly always described as "prostitution," the sacred women repeatedly referred to as "temple prostitutes" or "ritual prostitutes." The use of the word "prostitute" as a translation for *qadishtu* not only negates the sanctity of that which was held sacred, but suggests, by the inferences and social implications of the word, an ethnocentric subjectivity on the part of the writer. It leads the reader to a misinterpretation of the religious beliefs and social structure of the period. It seems to me that the word "prostitute" entirely distorts the very meaning of the ancient customs which the writer is supposedly explaining.[13]

Healing Sexual Relationships

If any degree of sexual healing has occurred in the West since the sexual revolution of the sixties, it has occurred *in spite of* rather than as a result of the sexual images with which the media constantly bombard us. Acceptance of sexuality as a spiritual power has nothing to do with the commercialized image of "sexiness" we are being pressured to conform to, leading to multimillion dollar sales for the industries involved. Unfortunately, the message of the mainstream commercial media is not that sexual pleasure is good, but rather that sexuality and pleasure are the special privilege of those who conform to certain standards of beauty and wealth. True sexual power depends not on certain looks or movements, but on self-acceptance and on the ability to open to deep levels of intimacy with another person.

Physical shame prevents us from experiencing our body and our lover's body as sacred, and our love-making as meditation and sacred action. We need to topple the dictatorship of shame and bring back the awareness of the sacred into sexuality. We need to realize that the division between physical and spiritual love is an artificial one. Both sexual and spiritual love belong to one single, continuous spectrum ranging from primitive, instinctual expressions of attraction to utterly sublime, selfless devotion. The power of attraction between two objects which we call gravity, springs from the same force which causes lovers to embrace. As the physicist Brian Swimme so aptly says, "The unity of the world rests on the pursuit of passion."[14]

Bringing Ecstasy Back into Worship

Any wall or boundary prevents movement in either direction. The barrier of shame separates the sexual from the spiritual; it not only keeps us from acknowledging our love-making as sacred action, but also bars Eros from entering our places of worship. Sex is no longer sacred, and worship is no longer erotic. Similarly, our relationship to God has lost the juice of ecstasy. Spiritual shame censors whatever erotic, sensual, or passionate feelings we might have toward the divine and prevents us from approaching God or Goddess as a being who loves us in intimate and physical ways.

Whenever we allow ourselves to pray though our entire being, we are involved in sacred dance. Sacred dance is a direct and utterly intimate expression of a person's innermost being. Through sacred dance, we relate to the divine through the totality of body, emotions, and spirit. Though it has often been said that the soul is naked before God, Western culture has tended to deny this powerfully erotic, emotional, and—from the perspec-

tive of our civilization—feminine aspect of spiritual practice. To call someone "shameless" is an insult, and yet, shameless is precisely what we need
to become in our love relationships, and above all in our relationship to
God. Finally, as the poet Kabir urged, we must cast off the protective
clothes and meet the Beloved with the full length of our body. The
sixteenth-century Indian saint Mirabai, herself one of the greatest devotional dancers of all times, repeats again and again that her love for
Krishna, whom she calls Shyam, "the dark one," has made her cast aside all
sense of shame:

> O my companion,
> I am dyed deep in the love of Shyam.
> I have donned anklets and ornaments
> And danced before Him without shame.[15]

In India, I was struck by the utter lack of inhibition with which adults
poured out their devotional feelings. I will never forget the performance of
a male dancer, who, while dancing before an audience of thousands, completely dissolved in devotional ecstasy and began to roll on the ground,
crying out the name of God. The audience responded in kind: people began to cry and pray. I, on the other hand, became aware of the deep sense
of shame surrounding my own devotional feelings. I, as many Westerners,
had always taken for granted that a person's religious feelings were a very
private affair. And yet, what power I saw released when shame is transcended! To witness the intimacy, intensity and immediacy of this dancer's
communion and lovemaking with God was indeed a great privilege.

Reclaiming the Sacred Lovers

Since the 1960 and 1970s, women have begun to reclaim the ancient image
of the Goddess. Though Western women are still abused and denied equality in so many ways, they have come a long way in healing themselves and
processing their anger. Yet just as women need to find the feminine form
of the divine, men also need to reclaim the male aspect of God for them-

selves. This is not an easy venture, considering the extent to that God, through patriarchy, has lost his tenderness, his erotic power, and his connection with nature. The overwhelming emphasis placed on masculinity in our culture, and the devaluation of the feminine has crippled and distorted both sexes. Through the men's movement, many men have begun to reclaim powers that were long denied them: sensitivity, compassion, earthiness, tenderness, playfulness. Ironically, all these are qualities that Jesus embodied in his actions and taught to his disciples, but that were later rejected as "unmanly." All these are attributes of the God-lover, of Pan, of Krishna, of Shiva, of Horus.

As the archetype of the divine lover reemerges, our images of both God and Goddess are transforming; their transformation is preparing the way toward a new sense of sacred relationship, a new image of the hieros gamos. Like the patriarchal God, the Goddess first reemerged in the 1970s as a single deity, not inclined to share her power equally with anyone, least of all a male. We create our deities in our own image, and so, the Goddess of the mid-twentieth century was bound to reflect the immense anger women had been forced to withhold for so long.

With the sacred lovers, an archetype that addresses both men and women and affirms their partnership has returned. Embodied spirit, they tell us of the sacredness of our own bodies, of the bodies of all living creatures, and of the earth. They awaken us to the emergence of ancient, yet timely forms of worship that involve the fullness of our passions and our bodies. They invite us to enter the dance of love with a deity as vulnerable and as dependent on us, as we on him or her—a god or goddess full of desire, waiting to be recognized and appreciated, who responds to our soul's call with equal passion. In our collective dreamings, such gods and goddesses—tender, erotic, and passionate—are beginning to appear, divine couples, co-creators of the world, who support the healing and wholeness of our own loving. This is the dream that today is inspiring the most profound expressions of art, song, dance, and celebration.

CHAPTER TEN: MEDITATIONS

Partner Meditation for Balancing the Chakras

Please read Chapter Eight and become familiar with the figure eight and its symbolism before doing this meditation. Also, read or practice *Moving with the Breath* (page 185), which outlines the basic pattern of breathing, and *The Symbol of Balance* (page 182), which illustrates the movement you will use. Review the illustration on page 101 to remind yourself of the location of the seven chakras.

Step One

Sit in a comfortable position, facing your partner at a distance of about two arms' lengths.

Begin to coordinate your breathing, so that you inhale and exhale together, pausing slightly after each inhalation and exhalation.

Focus on your first chakra and touch yourself lightly just above the pubic bone. Inhale and make an audible sigh on the next exhalation.

With the next inhalation, begin to draw the figure eight with both hands, as described in *Moving with the Breath* and *The Symbol of Balance,* coordinating the rhythm of your breath with your movements,

so that every downward slope of the figure eight is an exhalation and every upward slope an inhalation.

Although you are focusing on the first chakra, you need not hold your hands at that height. Rather, throughout the entire meditation your hands should be held wherever feels most natural and comfortable to you.

Both you and your partner begin by moving to the right. So as you move to the right, you should see your partner moving to your left.

Draw the figure eight in this way three times, feeling the energy within your own first chakra coming into balance. This will require six cycles of breath (six inhalations and exhalations).

Take one more inhalation and, making an audible sigh on the exhalation, refocus in your first chakra, again touching yourself lightly.

Next, imagine that the figure eight has pivoted, so that it now runs between you and your partner (see illustration), connecting you through the first chakra.

Again, you will both draw the figure eight three times, using the same breathing pattern.

And again, draw the symbol of balance with your hands. On the first inhalation, your palms are facing inward, moving up. On the exhalation, you follow the figure eight down and outward, your hands moving toward your partner.

On the second inhalation, your outstretched hands move upward, and on the second exhalation, they curve back down toward you, completing the first figure eight.

As you trace the figure eight between your own and your partner's first chakra, envision a profound balancing and healing taking place between you.

Again, use six breath cycles to draw the figure eight three times.

On the next breath cycle, move your focus up into the second chakra, the Hara, which lies about two inches below the navel center. Touch it and settle your consciousness in the Hara as you make an audible sigh on the exhalation.

Move through all the seven chakras in the same way, balancing them within yourself and between the two of you in this way. After you have completed the balancing practice at the crown chakra, sit quietly together for another minute or two, enjoying the harmonious energy that envelops you.

Step Two

Once you are both familiar with this meditation, you no longer need to use your hands at all but can simply visualize the figure eights as you breathe. At this stage, you can try doing this practice lying on your sides, facing each other and making sure you are both comfortable and can breathe easily.

Lying together allows you to feel the balancing and interconnecting of your energies that occurs during this practice in a very immediate and powerful way. Use this meditation before you make love, or at any time you feel the need to rebalance the relationship between yourself and your partner.

Dancing for the Inner Lover

RECOMMENDED MUSIC: Whatever music you enjoy

There are no rules in this process. But one thing is certain: the more intensity your call has, the clearer the response will be. Jesus told his followers to become like little children. If you have forgotten how to be childlike, start with sincerity. Sincerity dissolves the blockages. If you feel cynical, self-critical, or scared, sing and speak about it as you dance. Expressing the truth of the moment is opening the doorway to change.

> Choose the music that pleases you most, no matter if it is country-western or opera. And then, as Joseph Campbell said, follow your bliss. Put aside your shame, and dance your deepest love-longing. Dance for your inner lover as you would for the man or woman of your dreams.
>
> Know that in the eyes of your inner lover, you are exquisitely beautiful. Allow yourself to believe in a God or a Goddess who has chosen you for a lover, and who longs for you and desires you as intensely as you yourself might desire a lover. Let this sense of your own beauty and inner radiance expand as you dance.
>
> Push aside whatever comes in your way: furniture, phone calls, thoughts that say you are making a fool of yourself. Go ahead and dance! This is the best foolishness you will ever know.

RECOMMENDED MUSIC

THE FOLLOWING listings represent a sampling of my favorite music for movement meditation. By all means, use whatever appeals to you, including reggae, country, rock—whatever makes you want to move.

Some consumer-oriented stores are reintroducing the option of listening to music before purchasing it. If you are interested in acquiring music for movement meditation, I strongly recommend that you find out whether there are stores in your neighborhood offering any such options.

The first category includes tapes that are mainly rhythmic, while the music in the second category is more inward and quiet in nature. Of course, there is some overlap. All information refers to cassette recordings, although much of the following music is available on compact disc as well.

RHYTHMIC MUSIC

At the Edge. Mickey Hart with Jerry Garcia, Zakir Hussain, Olatunji, and others. RACS 0124 (RYKODISC).
Creative and masterful percussion play.

Double Drumming for the Shamanic Journey. Shamanic Journeywork Tape Series, No. 5, The Foundation for Shamanic Studies, Box 670, Belden Station, Norwalk, CT 06852.
Monotonous drumbeat, no variation throughout the entire tape.

The Dreamtime. Foday Musa Suso. CMP Records, CMP 3001 CS.
Rhythmic yet gentle and enchanting African music played on the *kora* (African harp-lute).

Earth Dreaming Dance. James Harvey and Tom Wasinger, INV 351. Invincible Productions, P.O. Box 13054, Phoenix, AZ 85002.

Wonderful trancelike dance music with the Australian Aboriginal *yidaki,* or *didgeridu.*

Earth Tribe Rhythms: A Total Drum Experience. 1990 Brent Lewis Productions, Tel. (213) 876-5625.

Remarkable drumming with a Middle Eastern flavor—very danceable.

Gateways to the Sun. Bente Friend. P.O. Box 1445, Santa Fe, NM 87504.

Rattles and drums to accompany the shamanic trance journey. The rattling is very constant and monotonous throughout the tape, which makes it an unlikely choice for normal listening but all the more useful for movement and trance work.

Handdance: Frame Drum Music. Glen Velez and Layne Redmond. Music of the World H 301, P.O. Box 258, Brooklyn, NY 11209.

Also by Glen Velez: **Ramana,** Music of the World H 307.

Healing Session with Babatunde Olatunji. KMA 85.

Olatunji is one of the greatest contemporary African drummers, and this is an excellent recording.

Journey of the Drums. Prem Das, Muruga, and Shakti. Musart Co., P.O. Box 20968, Oakland, CA 94619.

This is an exceptional drumming tape, with the additional advantage of including unusually long pieces.

Passion: Sources. WOMAD Production, Real World Records #91299-4.

Inspiring and passionate music from the Middle East.

Totem. Gabrielle Roth and the Mirrors. The Moving Center, P.O. Box 2034, Red Bank, NJ 07701.

Gabrielle Roth calls herself an urban shaman. Her music is urban, somewhat punk, and good for unbridled dancing. I also recommend her album **Initiation,** another Moving Center production.

MEDITATIVE MUSIC

Apollo. Brian Eno with Daniel Lanois and Roger Eno. EG Records Ltd., #ENOC 5.

One of my favorites—music for drifting in the outer reaches of inner space.

Celebration. Deuter. Kuckuck Records, Munich, Cassette MC 040.
Joyful and sweet.

Dream Passage. Daniel Kobialka DK 101. 1982 LiSem Enterprises, 1775 Old County Road #9, Belmont, CA 94002.
New Age orchestral versions of Kobialka's own compositions, as well as those of Vivaldi.

The Emerald Season. Piano Solos by Carolyn Margrete. Sunburst Music, 1442A Walnut Street, Rm. 366, Berkeley, CA 94709.
Dreamy, very beautiful piano pieces.

The Gyuto Monks: Tibetan Tantric Choir. Windham Hill, WT 2001.
The mystical sound of Tibetan monks chanting in an uncommonly deep, resonant voice.

Jewel. Michael Stearns. Sonic Atmospheres #208. 14755 Ventura Blvd., Suite 1776, Sherman Oaks, CA 91403.
Jungle sounds, bells, chanting. Good background for meditative practice.

Machu Picchu Impressions. Rusty Crutcher. Emerald Green Sound Productions, EG 8601, P.O. Box 16144, Santa Fe, NM 87506-6144.
Exquisite musical reflections on nature. One of my favorites.

Music of Keur Mousa. Sacred Spirit Music, P.O. Box 300, Shaker Road, New Lebanon, NY 12125.
Chants sung by monks of Keur Mousa, Senegal; a blend of traditional African rhythms and instruments with Christian church music.

Musique Soufi. Kudsi Erguner and Nezih Uzel, GREM records, #DMC 503-1 (record).
Ecstatic music of the whirling dervishes.

The Mystery Within. Janet Bray and Edie Hartshorne, Recorded in Grace Cathedral, San Francisco. Sacred Arts 201, 1173 Hearst Ave., Berkeley, CA 94702.
Highly recommended; quiet and very meditative.

One Hand Clapping. N. O. W. Records 4-126, distributed by: In the Light, 1647 Oceanfront Walk, Suite 7, Santa Monica, CA 90401.
Tibetan singing bells overlaid with nature sounds such as rippling water. This selection is exquisite—great for subtle movement work.

Overtone Chanting Meditations. Jill Purce, 20 Willow Road, London NW3, ENGLAND.
Hypnotic group chanting.

Parveen Sultana. Enchanting Bhajans. Oriental Records BGRP 1034, P.O. Box 1802, Grand Central Station, New York, NY 10017.

Indian devotional songs sung with the voice of a nightingale—high and very sweet.

Quiet Heart. Richard Warner, C 241. Antiquity Records, distributed by Music Design, Inc., 207 E. Buffalo, Milwaukee, WI 53202.

Beautiful meditative pieces on the bamboo flute.

Raindreaming. Gwen Jones and Kayla Kirsch. Raindreaming Productions, P.O. Box 2221, Berkeley, CA 94702.

New Age music for movement meditation.

Structures from Silence. Steve Roach. Fortuna Records, FOR #024, P.O. Box 1116, Novato, CA 94948.

Tranquil, synthesized music ideal for slow movement meditations.

Wind Chimes of the Mind. Katherine Wersen, 66436 12th Street #A, Desert Hot Springs, CA 92240.

Much like **One Hand Clapping.** Inward, meditative soundscapes with Tibetan bells and chimes.

REFERENCES

Jalaluddin Rumi. *We Are Three.* Translated by Coleman Barks. Athens, GA: May-pop Books, 1987, p. 68.

INTRODUCTION

Opening Quotation: Jalaluddin Rumi. *This Longing.* Translated by John Moyne and Coleman Barks. Putney, VT: Threshold Books, 1988, p. 55.

CHAPTER ONE

Opening Quotation: "The Marriage of Heaven and Hell." *The Complete Poetry & Prose of William Blake,* edited by David V. Erdman. New York: Anchor Press, 1988, p. 34.

1. *News of the Universe: poems of twofold consciousness.* Chosen and introduced by Robert Bly. San Francisco: Sierra Club Books, 1980, p. 212.

2. Brahadaranyaka Upanishad 1.4 1–5., found in: Joseph Campbell. *The Masks of God: Primitive Mythology.* New York: Penguin, 1987, p. 105.

3. Paramahansa Yogananda. *Man's Eternal Quest.* Los Angeles, CA: Self-Realization Fellowship, 1982, p. 366f.

4. Namkhai Norbu. *The Crystal and the Way of Light.* New York: Routledge & Kegan Paul, 1986, p. 126.

5. Ibid., p. 128.

6. Rosemary Radford Ruether, "Patristic Spirituality and the Experience of

Women in the Early Church," in: *Western Spirituality.* Edited by Matthew Fox. Santa Fe, NM: Bear & Co., 1981, p. 145.

7. See Chapter 10, footnotes 1 and 2.

8. Merlin Stone. *When God Was a Woman.* New York: Harvest/HBJ, 1976, p. 9f.

9. Ibid., p. 214f.

10. Elaine Pagels. *The Gnostic Gospels.* New York: Random House, 1979, p. 57.

11. Ibid., p. 63.

12. Chrystostomos, quoted in: Kaye Hoffman. *Tanz, Trance, Transformation.* Munich, Germany: Knaur Verlag, undated, p. 152 (author's translation).

13. Margeret Taylor, "A History of Symbolic Movement in Worship" in: *Dance as Religious Studies,* edited by Doug Adams and Diane Apostolos-Cappadona. New York: Crossroad, 1990, p. 29.

14. Kaye Hoffman. *Tanz, Trance, Transformation.* Munich, Germany: Knaur Verlag, undated, pp. 154–157.

15. *Grimm's Fairy Tales.* Translated by E. V. Lucas, Lucy Crane and Marian Edwardes. New York: Grosset & Dunlap, undated, p. 1.

16. Matthew Fox. *The Coming of the Cosmic Christ.* San Francisco: Harper & Row, p. 217.

17. Ken Wilber. *The Spectrum of Consciousness.* Wheaton, IL: Theosophical Publishing House, 1982, p. 33.

18. Fritjof Capra. *The Tao of Physics.* Boulder, CO: Shambhala, 1983, p. 131.

19. Ibid., p. 138.

CHAPTER TWO

Opening Quotation: Kabir. *The Kabir Book.* Versions by Robert Bly. Boston, MA: Beacon Press, 1971, 1977, p. 57.

1. J. Krishnamurti. *Talks with American Students.* Boulder, CO: Shambhala, 1988, p. 9.

2. Thich Nhat Hanh. *Being Peace.* Berkeley, CA: Parallax Press, 1987, p. 17.

3. Gabrielle Roth. *Maps to Ecstasy.* San Rafael, CA: New World Library, 1989, p. 9.

CHAPTER THREE

Opening Quotations: Wu-Men, from *The Enlightened Heart.* Stephen Mitchell. New York: Harper & Row Publishers, 1989, p. 47.

Lao Tsu. *Tao Te Ching.* Translated from the Chinese by Gia-Fu Feng and Jane English. New York: Vintage Book Edition, 1972, Verse 16.

Ts'ai-ken t'an, quoted in: T. Legett. *A First Zen Reader.* Rutland, VT: C. E. Tuttle, 1972, p. 29.

1. Paramahansa Yogananada. *Autobiography of a Yogi.* Los Angeles, CA: Self-Realization Fellowship, 1987, pp. 260ff.

2. Peter Matthiessen. *Nine-Headed Dragon River.* Boston, MA: Shambhala, 1987, p. 82.

3. Gretel Ehrlich. *The Solace of Open Spaces.* New York: Penguin, 1985, pp. 14–15.

4. Letter to Countess Margot Sizzo-Noris-Crouy, January 6, 1923, in: *The Sonnets to Orpheus.* Translated by Stephen Mitchell. New York: Touchstone, 1986, p. 166.

5. Thich Nhat Hanh. *Being Peace.* Berkeley, CA: Parallax Press, 1987, p. 5.

6. *The Jerusalem Bible.* Garden City, NY: Doubleday & Co., 1968.

CHAPTER FOUR

Opening Quotation: Uvavnuk. From *Touch the Earth: A Self-Portrait of Indian Existence.* T. C. McLuhan. New York: Simon & Schuster, 1971, p. 25.

1. Arnold Mindell. *Dreambody.* Boston, MA: Sigo Press, 1982, p. 90.

2. Acts of John 101, in: Hennecke-Schneemelcher, *New Testament Apocrypha* (translated from the German, *Neutestamentliche Apokryphen*), Philadelphia, 1964, volume 2.232.

3. Thich Nhat Hanh. *The Miracle of Mindfulness.* Boston, MA: Beacon Press, 1976, p. 23.

4. Kabir. *The Kabir Book.* Versions by Robert Bly, p. 33.

5. For a diagram of the seven main chakras, see p. 99.

6. Matthew Fox. *The Coming of the Cosmic Christ*. San Francisco: Harper & Row, p. 133.

7. Jean Houston. *The Possible Human: A Course in Extending Your Physical, Mental, and Creative Abilities*. Los Angeles, CA: J. P. Tarcher, 1982, p. 187.

8. Thich Nhat Hanh. *Being Peace*. Berkeley, California: Parallax Press, 1987, p. 23.

CHAPTER FIVE

Opening Quotation: Karlfried Graf Durckheim. *Hara: The Vital Centre of Man*. London: Unwin Hyman Ltd., pp. 176–177.

1. The story of Prince Lindworm, the serpent-man, retold by Joseph L. Henderson and Maud Oakes. *The Wisdom of the Serpent*. Princeton, NJ: Princeton University Press, 1990, pp. 167–172.

2. Joanna Macy. *Despair and Personal Power in the Nuclear Age*. Philadelphia, PA: New Society Publishers, 1983, p. 22.

3. A good introduction is Rosalyn Bruyere's *Wheels of Light: A Study of the Chakras*. Sierra Madre, CA: Bon Productions, 1989.

4. *Emmanuel's Book II*. Compiled by Pat Rodegast and Judith Stanton. New York: Bantam, 1989, p. 28.

5. Mircea Eliade. *The Sacred & The Profane: The Nature of Religion*. San Diego, CA: A Harvest Harcourt Brace Jovanovich Book, 1959, pp. 64f.

CHAPTER SIX

Opening Quotation: Joseph Campbell. *The Power of Myth*. New York: Doubleday, 1988, p. 47.

1. Lao Tsu. *Tao Te Ching*. Translated from the Chinese by Gia-Fu Feng and Jane English. New York: Vintage Book Edition, 1972, Verse 42.

2. Buffie Johnson. *Lady of the Beasts*. San Francisco: Harper & Row, 1988, pp. 121–184.

3. Barbara Walker. *The Woman's Encyclopedia of Myths and Secrets*. San Francisco: Harper & Row, 1983, p. 904.

4. Joseph Campbell. *The Masks of God: Occidental Mythology*. New York: Viking Penguin, 1976, p. 25.

5. Ibid., p. 26.

6. Ibid.

7. Merlin Stone. *When God Was a Woman,* pp. 198f.

8. Gopi Krishna. *Kundalini: The Evolutionary Energy in Man.* Boulder, CO and London: Shambhala, 1971.

9. Ibid., p. 153.

10. Kaye Hoffman. *Tanz, Trance, Transformation.* Munich, Germany: Knaur Verlag, undated, p. 42.

11. Riane Eisler. *The Chalice & The Blade.* San Francisco: Harper & Row, 1987, p. xvii.

CHAPTER SEVEN

Opening Quotations: Maya Deren. *Divine Horsemen: The Living Gods of Haiti.* New York: Documentext, McPherson & Co, 1970, p. 238.

Yaya Diallo and Mitchell Hall. *The Healing Drum.* Rochester, VT: Destiny Books, 1989, p. 109.

1. Arnold Mindell. *Working on Yourself Alone: Inner Dreambody Work.* London: Penguin/Arkana, 1990, p. 43.

2. Dorothy Maclean. *To Hear the Angels Sing.* Issaquah, WA: Lorian Press, 1980, p. 165.

3. Rainer Maria Rilke. *Letters to a Young Poet.* Translated by M. D. Herter Norton. New York: W. W. Norton & Co., 1954, p. 38.

4. Yaya Diallo and Mitchell Hall. *The Healing Drum.* Rochester, VT: Destiny Books, 1989, pp. 116f.

5. Chögyam Trungpa. *Shambhala: The Sacred Path of the Warrior.* Boston, MA: Bantam Books, 1986, p. 20.

6. Yaya Diallo and Mitchell Hall. *The Healing Drum.* Rochester, VT: Destiny Books, 1989, p. 79.

7. Reinhard Flatischler. *Die vergessene Macht des Rhythmus,* copyright © 1984 by Synthesis Verlag, Essen, Germany, 1984, p. 19. Jalaja Bonheim's translation printed by permission.

8. Matthew Fox. *The Coming of the Cosmic Christ*. San Francisco: Harper & Row, p. 133.

9. Yaya Diallo and Mitchell Hall. *The Healing Drum*. Rochester, VT: Destiny Books, 1989, p. 150.

CHAPTER EIGHT

Opening Quotation: Jalaluddin Rumi. In *Open Secret: Versions of Rumi*. Coleman Barks and John Moyne. Putney, VT: Threshold Books, 1984, Quattrain 158.

1. *The Rhineland Mystics*. Edited, introduced, and translated by Oliver Davies. New York: Crossroad, 1990, p. 61.

2. Namkhai Norbu. *The Crystal and the Way of Light*. New York: Routledge & Kegan Paul, 1986, p. 86.

3. Alan Watts. *Diamond Web: Live in the Moment*. Selected Lectures, edited by Mark Watts. South Bend, IN: and Books, 1987, p. 147.

4. Fritjof Capra. *The Tao of Physics*. Boulder, CO: Shambhala, 1983, p. 106.

5. Thich Nhat Hanh. *The Heart of Understanding*. Berkeley, CA: Parallax Press, 1988, p. 31f.

6. Lao Tsu. *Tao Te Ching*. Translated from the Chinese by Gia-Fu Feng and Jane English. New York: Vintage Book Edition, 1972, Verse 2.

7. This is true of both hetero- and homosexual lovemaking, since every human being possesses both masculine and feminine energies.

8. Thich Nhat Hanh. *Being Peace*. Berkeley, California: Parallax Press, 1987, p. 5.

9. Fritjof Capra. *The Tao of Physics*. Boulder, CO: Shambhala, 1983, p. 154.

10. Barbara Myerhoff. "Shamanic Equilibrium: Balance and Meditation in Known and Unknown Worlds," in: *American Folk Medicine: A Symposium,* edited by Wayland D. Hand. Berkeley, CA: University of California Press, 1980, pp. 100–101.

CHAPTER NINE

Opening Quotations: Lao Tsu. *Tao Te Ching*. Translated from the Chinese by Gia-Fu Feng and Jane English. New York: Vintage Book Edition, 1972, Verse 56.

"The Odes of Solomon." From *The Enlightened Heart*. Stephen Mitchell. New York: Harper & Row Publishers, 1989, p. 24.

1. Chögyam Trungpa. *The Myth of Freedom and the Way of Meditation.* Boulder, CO: Shambhala, 1976, p. 113.

2. Thich Nhat Hanh. *A Guide to Walking Meditation.* Nyack, NY: Fellowship Publication Books, 1985.

3. Peace Pilgrim. *Peace Pilgrim: Her Life and Work in Her Own Words.* Santa Fe, NM: An Ocean Tree Book, 1983, p. 44.

4. Lao Tsu. *Tao Te Ching.* Translated from the Chinese by Gia-Fu Feng and Jane English. New York: Vintage Book Edition, 1972, Verse 29.

5. Thich Nhat Hanh. *A Guide to Walking Meditation.* Nyack, NY: Fellowship Publication Books, 1985.

CHAPTER TEN

Opening Quotation: Kabir. *The Kabir Book.* Versions by Robert Bly, p. 42.

1. *The Nag Hammadi Library.* Edited by James M. Robinson. San Francisco: Harper & Row, 1978, p. 218.

2. Ibid., p. 121.

3. Acts of John 95.12-17, in: Hennecke-Schneemelcher, *New Testament Apocrypha,* volume 2.229.

4. *Beguine Spirituality: Mystical Writings of Mechthild of Majdeburg, Beatrice of Nazareth and Hadewijch of Brabant,* edited and introduced by Fiona Bowie. New York: Crossroad, 1990, p. 57.

5. Frederique Apffel-Marglin. *Wives of the God-King: The Rituals of the Devadasis of Puri.* Oxford, England: Oxford University Press, 1985.

6. Enakshi Bhavnani. *The Dance in India.* Bombay: D.B. Taraporevala Sons & Co., 1965, p. 29.

7. Frederique Apffel-Marglin. *Wives of the God-King,* p. 203.

8. Ibid., p. 29.

9. Ibid., p. 315.

10. William Irwin Thompson. *The Time Falling Bodies Take to Light: Mythology, Sexuality, and the Origins of Culture.* New York: St. Martin's Press, 1981, p. 200.

11. Barbara Walker. *The Woman's Encyclopedia of Myths and Secrets.* San Francisco: Harper & Row, 1983, p. 821.

12. Nancy Qualls-Corbett. *The Sacred Prostitute.* Toronto, Canada: Inner City Books, 1988.

13. Merlin Stone. *When God Was a Woman.* New York: Harvest/HBJ, 1976, p. 157.

14. Brian Swimme. *The Universe Is a Green Dragon: A Cosmic Creation Story.* Santa Fe, NM: Bear & Co., 1984, p. 48.

15. *The Devotional Poems of Mirabai.* Translated by A. J. Alston. Delhi: Motilal Banarsidass, 1980, p. 40.

INDEX

Other Books You May Enjoy . . .

Beginner's Tai Ji Book *by Chungliang Al Huang*
The foundations of Tai Ji, presented by one of the world's foremost authorities. The brief lessons are illustrated with beautiful color photographs, and often appear in the form of a story, poem, or mind/body exercise. To work with this book is to experience the wonder and delight of studying with a great teacher.
$12.95 paper, 96 pages

Embrace Tiger, Return to Mountain
by Chungliang Al Huang
Huang's philosophical interpretations of Tai Ji are widely known and respected. His unique insight is the result of a deep yet playful understanding of Eastern tradition, coupled with years of professional training in dance and martial arts.
$12.95 paper, 256 pages

Crazy Wisdom *by Wes "Scoop" Nisker*
This glorious romp through human history celebrates the fools, prophets, madmen, and teachers who have found wisdom on the other side of convention. Lighthearted lessons are punctuated with quotes from crazy wisdom practitioners like Chuang Tzu, Jesus Christ, Mark Twain, and Albert Einstein. A TEN SPEED PRESS BOOK
$12.95, 240 pages

The Common Book of Consciousness *Revised Edition*
by Diana Saltoon
A beloved sourcebook, newly updated for the 1990s. This guide to leading a whole and centered life shows how to use meditation, exercise, and nutrition to gain a higher consciousness and a full, balanced daily life.
$11.95 paper, 160 pages

May we suggest classics on tape from Audio Literature . . .

Tao Te Ching *translated by Gia-fu Feng and Jane English*
Philosopher and author Jacob Needleman reads one of the world's most revered sources of spiritual wisdom. *$15.95, 2 hours and 15 minutes*

Poems of Rumi
translated and read by Robert Bly and Coleman Barks
The words of the great poet and Islamic saint are accompanied by sitar, tabla, flute, and percussion in this powerful presentation.
$15.95, 2 hours and 30 minutes

Like This: More Poems of Rumi
translated and read by Coleman Barks
An intense collaboration between the music of Hamza El-Din and the cherished words of Jallaludin Rumi. *$10.95, 1 hour and 23 minutes*

Poems of Kabir *translated and read by Robert Bly*
Backed by tabla and sitar, acclaimed poet Robert Bly recites the extraordinary religious poetry of the 15th-century Indian sage. *$15.95, 2 hours*

The Dhammapada
translated by Thomas Byron, read by Jack Kornfield
The sayings of the Buddha in this sacred text have guided countless people in their search for inner transformation. *$9.95, 1 hour and 14 minutes*

The Bhagavad-Gita *translated by Barbara Stoler Miller*
Jacob Needleman reads India's most precious gift to seekers of spiritual truth. *$15.95, 2 hours and 29 minutes*

Celestial Arts
Box 7327
Berkeley, CA 94707
(510) 845-8414

Available from your local bookstore, or order direct from the publisher. Please include $1.25 shipping & handling for the first book, and 50 cents for each additional book. California residents include local sales tax. Write for our free complete catalog of over 400 books and tapes.